The Iron Chest: a play. The second edition. [Based on William Godwin's novel "Things as they are."] MS. alterations.

George Colman

The Iron Chest: a play ... The second edition. [Based on William Godwin's novel "Things as they are."] MS. alterations.

Colman, George
British Library, Historical Print Editions
British Library
1798
109 p. ; 8°.
643.h.13.(4.)

The BiblioLife Network

This project was made possible in part by the BiblioLife Network (BLN), a project aimed at addressing some of the huge challenges facing book preservationists around the world. The BLN includes libraries, library networks, archives, subject matter experts, online communities and library service providers. We believe every book ever published should be available as a high-quality print reproduction; printed on- demand anywhere in the world. This insures the ongoing accessibility of the content and helps generate sustainable revenue for the libraries and organizations that work to preserve these important materials.

The following book is in the "public domain" and represents an authentic reproduction of the text as printed by the original publisher. While we have attempted to accurately maintain the integrity of the original work, there are sometimes problems with the original book or micro-film from which the books were digitized. This can result in minor errors in reproduction. Possible imperfections include missing and blurred pages, poor pictures, markings and other reproduction issues beyond our control. Because this work is culturally important, we have made it available as part of our commitment to protecting, preserving, and promoting the world's literature.

GUIDE TO FOLD-OUTS, MAPS and OVERSIZED IMAGES

In an online database, page images do not need to conform to the size restrictions found in a printed book. When converting these images back into a printed bound book, the page sizes are standardized in ways that maintain the detail of the original. For large images, such as fold-out maps, the original page image is split into two or more pages.

Guidelines used to determine the split of oversize pages:

• Some images are split vertically; large images require vertical and horizontal splits.
• For horizontal splits, the content is split left to right.
• For vertical splits, the content is split from top to bottom.
• For both vertical and horizontal splits, the image is processed from top left to bottom right.

THE

IRON CHEST:

A

PLAY.

[PRICE TWO SHILLINGS.]

THE

IRON CHEST:

A PLAY;

IN THREE ACTS.

WRITTEN BY

GEORGE COLMAN,

THE YOUNGER.

FIRST REPRESENTED AT THE THEATRE ROYAL DRURY-
LANE, ON SATURDAY, 12TH MARCH, 1796.

THE THIRD EDITION.

LONDON:

PRINTED BY T. WOODFALL,

FOR MESSRS. CADELL AND DAVIES,

IN THE STRAND.

1798.

DRAMATIS PERSONÆ.

Sir Edward Mortimer, ... *Mr. Kemble.*
Fitzharding, ... *Mr. Wroughton.*
Wilford, ... *Mr. Bannister jun.*
Adam Winterton, ... *Mr. Dodd.*
Rawbold, ... *Mr. Barrymore.*
Samson, ... *Mr. Suett.*
Boy, ... *Master Welsh.*
Cook, ... *Mr. Hollingsworth.*
Peter, ... *Mr. Banks.*
Walter, ... *Mr. Maddocks.*
Simon, ... *Mr. Webb.*
Gregory, ... *Mr. Trueman.*
Armstrong, ... *Mr. Kelly.*
Orson, ... *Mr. R. Palmer.*
1st Robber, ... *Mr. Dignum.*
2d Robber, ... *Mr. Sedgwick.*
3d Robber, ... *Mr. Bannister.*
Robber's Boy, ... *Master Welb.*

Helen, ... *Miss Farren.*
Blanch, ... *Mrs. Gibbs.*
Dame Rawbold, ... *Miss Tidswell.*
Barbara, ... *Signora Storace.*
Judith, ... *Miss De Camp.*

SCENE, *in the New Forest, in Hampshire, and*
on its Borders.

THE IRON CHEST;

A PLAY,

IN THREE ACTS.

ACT I.—SCENE I.

The inside of RAWBOLD'S COTTAGE. *Several children, squalid and beggarly, discovered in different parts of the room: some asleep.* DAME RAWBOLD *seated, leaning over the embers of the fire.* BARBARA *seated near her.* SAMSON *standing in the front of the stage. A narrow stair-case in the back scene. A taper burning. The whole scene exhibits poverty and wretchedness.*

GLEE.

SAMSON.

FIVE times, by the taper's light,
The hour-glass I have turn'd to night.
First Boy. Where's father?
Samson. He's gone out to roam:
If he have luck,
He'll bring a buck,
Upon his lusty shoulders, home.

       The different voices.

Home! home!
He comes not home!

B

Hark!

Hark! from the woodland vale below,
The diftant clock founds, dull, and flow!
Bome! bome! bome!

Sam. Five o'clock, and father not yet returned from New Foreft! An he come not fhortly,
the Sun will rife, and roaft the venifon on his
fhoulders.—Sifter Barbara!—Well, your rich men
have no bowels for us lowly! they little think,
while they are gorging on the fat haunch of a
goodly buck, what fatigues we poor honeft fouls
undergo in ftealing it.—Why, fifter Barbara!

Bar. I am here, brother Sampfon. (*getting up*).

Sam. Here!—marry, out upon you for an idle
baggage! why, you crawl like a fnail.

Bar. I prithee, now, do not chide me, Samfon!

Sam. 'Tis my humour. I am father's head
man in his poaching. The rubs I take from him,
who is above me, I hand down to you, who are
below me. 'Tis the way of office—where every
miferable devil domineers it over the next more
miferable devil that's under him. You may
fcold fifter Margery, an you will—fhe's your
younger by a twelvemonth.

Bar. Truly, brother, I would not make any
one unhappy, for the world. I am content to do
what I can to pleafe, and to mind the houfe.

Sam. Truly, a weighty matter! Thou art e'en
ready to hang thyfelf, for want of fomething to
while away time. What haft thou much more
to do than to trim the faggots, nurfe thy mother,
boil the pot, patch our jackets, kill the poultry,
cure the hogs, feed the pigs, and comb the children?

Bar. Many might think that no fmall charge,
Samfon.

Sam.

Sam. A mere nothing.—While father and I (bate us but the mother and children) have the credit of purloining every single thing that you have the care of. We are up early, and down late, in the exercise of our industry.

Bar. I wish father, and you, would give up the calling.

Sam. No—there is one keen argument to prevent us.

Bar. What's that, brother?

Sam. Hunger. Wouldst have us be rogues, and let our family starve? Give up poaching and deer-stealing! Oons! dost think we have no conscience? Yonder sits mother, poor soul—old, helpless, and crazy.

Bar. Alas! brother, 'tis heart-aching to look upon her. This very time three years she got her maim. It was a piteous tempest!

Sam. Aye—'twas rough weather.

Bar. I never pass the old oak, that was shivered that night, in the storm, but I am ready to weep. It remembers me of the time when all our poor family went to ruin.

Sam. Pish—no matter: The cottage was blown down—the barn fired—father undone—Well, landlords are flinty hearted—no help! what then? We live, don't we? (*sullenly*).

Bar. Troth, brother, very sadly. Father has grown desperate; all is fallen to decay. We live by pilfering on the Forest—and our poor mother distracted, and unable to look to the house. The rafter, which fell in the storm, struck so heavy upon her brain, I fear me 'twill never again be settled.

Moth. Children! Barbara! where's my eldest daughter? She is my darling.

Bar.

Bar.   I am here, mother.

Sam.   Peace, fool! you know she's doating.

Moth.   Look to the cattle, Barbara! We must to market to-morrow.   My husband's a rich man, We thrive! we thrive! Ha, ha, ha!—oh!

Bar.   Oh brother! I cannot bear to see her thus—though, alas! we have long been used to it.   The little ones too—scarce cloath'd—hungry —almost starving!—Indeed, we are a very wretched family.

Sam.   Hark! Methought I heard a tread.— Hist! be wary.   We must not open in haste, for fear of surprises.

(*A knock at the Cottage door.*)

DUET.

Samson.   Who knocks at this dead hour?
Rawbold (without.)   A friend.
Samson.   How should we know,
        A friend from foe?
    A signal you must give.
Rawbold (without.)   Attend.

(*Rawbold gives three knocks, which Samson counts, singing at intervals.*)

Samson.   ——One, two, three!
            'Tis he.
    Give me the word we fixt to night.
    'Tis Roebuck (*in a whisper to Barbara*)
Rawbold (without.)   Roebuck.
Samson.   That is right,
        Enter now by candle-light.
Rawbold.   Open now by candle light.

Samsom *opens the door,* and Rawbold *enters.*

Raw.   Bar the door.   So, softly.

Sam.   What success, father?

Raw.   Good: my limbs ache for't.

Moth.   O brave husband! Welcome from the
                                court.

court. Thou fhalt be made a knight; and I a
lady. Ha! ha!

Raw. Reft, reft, poor foul!—How you ftand!
(*to Sampfon*). The chair, you gander!

Sam (*to Barbara*) Why how you ftand! the
chair, you gander!

(*They bring Rawbold a chair: he fits.*

Raw. Here—take my gun—'tis unfcrewed.
The keepers are abroad. I had fcarce time to get
it in my pocket.

(*He pulls the gun from a pocket under his coat, in
three pieces, which Samfon fcrews together, while
they are talking.*)

Fie! 'tis fharp work! Barbara, you jade, come
hither.

Sam. Barbara, you jade, come hither.

Raw. Who bid thee chide her, lout! Kifs thy
old father, wench. Kifs me, I fay.—So—why doft
tremble? I am rough as a tempeft. Evil fortune
has blown my lowring nature into turbulence:
but thou art a bloffom that doft bend thy head fo
fweetly under my gufts of paffion, 'tis pity they
fhould e'er harm thee.

Bar. Indeed, father, I am glad to fee you fafe
returned.

Raw. I believe thee. Take the keys. Go to
the locker, in the loft, and bring me a glafs to
recruit me. (*Barbara goes out.*

Sam. Well, father, and fo————

Raw. Peace.—I ha' fhot a buck.

Sam. O rare! Of all the fure aims, on the
borders of the New Foreft; here, give me old
Gilbert Rawbold; though I, who am his fon, fay
it, that fhould not fay it.—Where have you ftow'd
him, father?

Raw. Under the furze, behind the hovel.

Come

Come night again, we will draw him in, boy.   I
have been watch'd.

Sam.   Watch'd ! O, the peſtilence ! our trade
will be ſpoiled if the Groom Keepers be after us.
The law will perſecute us, father.

Raw.   Do'ſt know Mortimer !

Sam.   What, Sir Edward Mortimer ? Aye, ſure.
He is head Keeper of the foreſt.   'Tis he who has
ſhut himſelf up in melancholy.   Sees no rich, and
does ſo much good to the poor.

Raw.   He has done me naught but evil.   A
gun cannot be carried on the border, here, but he
has ſcent on't, at a league's diſtance.   He is a thorn
to me.   His ſcouts this night were after me—all
on the watch.   I'll he revenged—I'll—So, the
brandy.—*Enter* BARBARA, *with the Liquor.*

Raw. (after drinking) 'Tis right, ifaith !

Sam.   That 'tis I'll be ſworn ; for I ſmuggled
it myſelf.   We do not live ſo near the coaſt for
nothing.

Raw.   Sir Edward Mortimer look to it !

Barb.   Sir Edward Mortimer ! O, dear father,
what of him ?

Raw.   Aye, now thou art all agog !   Thou
woud'ſt hear ſomewhat of that ſmooth-tongued
fellow, his ſecretary—his clerk, Wilford ; whom
thou ſo often meet'ſt in the foreſt.   I have news
on't.   Look how you walk thither again.   What,
thou wouldſt betray me to him, I warrant ;—conſpire againſt your father.

Sam.   Aye ! conſpire againſt you father—and
your tender loving brother, you viper, you !

Barb.   Beſhrew me, father, I meant no harm :
and, indeed, indeed, Wilford is as handſome a—
I mean as good a youth as ever breathed.   If I
thought he meant ill by you, I ſhould hate him.

Raw.

Raw. When didſt ſee him laſt?—Speak!

Barb. You terrify me ſo, father, I am ſcarce able to ſpeak. Yeſternoon, by the copſe: 'Twas but to read with him the book of ſonnets, he gave me.

Sam. That's the way your ſly, grave rogues, work into the hearts of the females. I never knew any good come of a girl's reading ſonnets, with a learned clerk, under a copſe.

Raw. Let me hear no more of your meetings. I am content to think you would not plot my undoing.

Barb. I?—O father!

Raw. But he may plot yours. Mark me—Fortune has thruſt me forth to prowl, like the wolf;—but the wolf is anxious for its young. I am an outcaſt whom hunger has hardened. I violate the law; but feeling is not dead within me: and, callous villain as I am accounted, I would tear that greater villain piecemeal, who would violate my child, and rob an old man of the little remains of comfort wretchedneſs has left him.

(*A knocking at the door. A voice without.*
Hilliho! ho!)

Raw. How now!

Sam. There! an they be not after us already. I'll—We have talk'd, too, 'till 'tis broad day light.

Wilford (*without*). Open, good maſter Rawbold; I would ſpeak to you ſuddenly.

Barb. O heaven! 'tis the voice of Wilford himſelf.

Raw. Wilford! I'm glad on't—Now he ſhall—I'm glad on't. Open the door: Quickly, I ſay—He ſhall ſmart for it.

Sam.

Sam. Are you mad, father? 'Tis we shall smart for it. Let in the keeper's head man! The hind quarter of a buck has hung these fourteen days, in the pantry.

Raw. Open, I say.

Sam. O Lord! I defy any secretary's nose not to smell stolen venison the moment 'tis thrust into our hovel.

SAMSON *opens the door. Enter* WILFORD.

Wilf. Save you, good people! You are Gilbert Rawbold, as I take it.

Raw. I am. Your message here, young man bodes me no good: but I *am* Gilbert Rawbold—and here's my daughter. Do'st know her?

Wilf. Ah, Barbara, good wench! how fares it with you?

Raw. Look on her well—then consult your own conscience. 'Tis difficult, haply, for a secretary to find one. You are a villain.

Wilf. You lie.—Hold, I crave pardon. You are her father. She is innocent, and you are unhappy: I respect virtue and misfortune too much to shock the one or insult the other.

Raw. Sdeath! why meet my daughter in the forest?

Wilf. Because I love her.

Raw. And would ruin her.

Wilf. That's a strange way of shewing one's love, methinks. I have a simple notion, Gilbert, that the thought of having taken a base advantage of a poor girl's affection might go nigh to break a man's sleep, and give him unquiet dreams: now, I love my night's rest, and shall do nothing to disturb it.

                                        Raw.

Raw. Would'ſt not poiſon her mind?

Wiif. 'Tis not my method, friend, of doſing a patient. Look ye, Gilbert; Her mind is a fair flower, ſtuck in the rude ſoil, here, of ſurrounding ignorance, and ſmiling in the chill of poverty:—I would feign cheer it with the little ſun-ſhine I poſſeſs of comfort and information. My parents were poor like her's; Should occaſion ſerve, I might, haply, were all parties agreed, make her my wife. To offer ought elſe would affect her, you, and myſelf; and I have no talent at making three people uneaſy at the ſame time.

Raw. Your hand. On your own account, we are friends.

Barb. O dear father!

Raw. Be ſilent. Now to your errand. 'Tis from Mortimer.

Wiif. I come from Sir Edward.

Raw. I know his malice. He would oppreſs me with his power. He would ſtarve me, and my family. Search my houſe.

Samſ. No, father no! You forget the hind quarter in the pantry. (*aſide*)

Raw. Let him do his worſt: but let him beware. A tyrant; a villain!

Wilf. Harkye—he is my maſter. I owe him my gratitude;—every thing:—and had you been any but my Barbara's father, and ſpoken ſo much againſt him, my indignation had work'd into my knuckles, and cram'd the words down your ruſty throat.

Samſ. I do begin to perceive how this will end. Father will knock down the ſecretary, as flat as a buck.

Raw. Why am I ſingled out? Is there no mark for the vengeance of office to ſhoot its ſhaft

C at

at but me? This morning, as he dog'd me in the foreſt———

Wilf. Huſh, Rawbold. Keep your counſel. Should you make it publick he muſt notice it.

Raw. Did he not notice it?

Wilf. No matter—but he has ſent me thus early, Gilbert, with this relief to your diſtreſſes, which he has heard of. Here are twenty marks, for you, and your family.

Raw. From Sir Edward Mortimer?

Wilf. 'Tis his way;—but he would not have it mentioned. He is one of thoſe judges who, in their office, will never warp the law to ſave offenders: but his private charity bids him aſſiſt the needy, before their neceſſities drive them to crimes which his publick duty muſt puniſh.

Raw. Did Mortimer do this! did he! heaven bleſs him! Oh, young man, if you knew half the miſery—my wife—my children—Shame 'ont! I have ſtood many a tug, but the drops, now, fall in ſpite of me. I am not ungrateful; but I cannot ſtand it. We will talk of Barbara when I have more man about me.

(Exit up the ſtair-caſe.

Wilf. Farewell. I muſt home to the lodge quickly. Ere this, I warrant, I am looked for.

Barb. Farewell.

QUINTETTO.

Wilford.

THE Sun has tipt the hills with red;
The lout now flouriſhes his flail;
The punchy Parſon waddles from his bed,
Heavy, and heated, with his laſt night's ale.

Adieu!

Adieu! adieu! I muſt be going;
The dapper village cock is crowing.
    Adieu, my little Barbara!

Barbara.

Adieu!---and ſhould you think upon
The lowly cottage, when you're gone,
Where two old Oaks, with ivy deckt,
Their branches o'er the roof projeƈt,
I pray, good ſir, juſt recolleƈt
    That there lives little Barbara.

Samſon.

And Samſon too, good ſir, in ſmoke and ſmother;
Barbara's very tender---loving brother.

Firſt Boy, to Samſon.

Brother, look! the Sun, aloof,
Peeps through the crannies of the roof.
Give us food, good brother, pray!
For we eat nothing yeſterday.

Children.   Give us food, good brother, pray!
Samſon.   Oh, fire and faggot! what a ſqualling!
Barbara.   Do not chide 'em.-----
Samſon   Damn their bawling!
Hungry ſtomachs there's no balking:
I wiſh I could ſtop their mouths with talking:
But very good meat is, cent per cent,
Dearer than very good argument.

Wilford.   Adieu, adieu! I muſt be going;
           The dapper village cock is crowing.
               Adieu, my little Barbara!   }
Barbara.   Oh, think on little Barbara!   }
Children. Give us food!
Sampſon.   Curſe their ſqualling!
Wilford and Barbara.   Adieu! adieu!
Sampſon.   Damn their bawling!

Samſon, Wilford, and Barbara.

Adieu my little Barbara!   }
Oh, think on little Barbara!   }
You'll think on little Barbara.   }

C 2   SCENE

SCENE II. *An old fashion'd Hall, in* Sir Edward Mortimer's *Lodge.*

*Several Servants cross the Stage, with Flaggons,
Tankards, Cold meat, &c. &c.*

Enter Adam Winterton.

Wint. Softly, varlets, softly! See you crack
none of the stone flaggons. Nay, 'tis plain your
own breakfasts be toward, by your skuttling thus.
—A goodly morning! Why, you giddy-pated
knave, *(to one of the servants.)* is it so you carry a
dish of pottery? No heed of our good master's
Sir Edward Mortimer's ware? Fie, Peter Pick-
bone, fie!

Serv. I am in haste, master Steward, to break
my fast.

Wint. To break thy fast!—to break thy neck,
it should seem. Ha! ha' good i'faith!—Go thy
ways knave! *(Exit servant.)* 'Tis thus the
rogues ever have me. I would feign be angry
with them, but, straight, a merry jest passeth across
me, and my choler is over. To break thy neck
it should seem! ha, ha! 'twas well conceited, by
St. Thomas!——My table-book, for the business
of the day. Ah, my memory holds not as it did.
It needs the spur. *(Looking over his book.)* Nine
and forty years have I been house-steward, and
butler. Let me see.—Six winters ago, come
Christmas eve, died my old master, Sir Marmaduke.—Ah! he was a heavy loss. I look'd to
drop before him. He was hale and tough:—but,
thank heaven, I ha' seen him out, my dear old
master!—

master!—Let me see—my tables; (*Looking over them and singing.*

> When birds do carrol on the bush,
>   With a heigh no nonny——heigho!

Enter Cook.

Cook. Master Steward! Good master Winterton!

Wint. Who calls merry old Adam Winterton? Ha, Jacob Cook! Well bethought—the dinner. Nay, I bear a brain: thinking men will combine. I never see Jacob Cook but it reminds me of ordering dinner. We must have——what say my tables?——we must have, Jacob——Nay, by St. Thomas, I perceive 'twas Christmas eve *seven* years died my good old master, sir Marmaduke.

Cook. I pray you despatch me, good master steward. I would bestir in time.

Wint. Then I would counsel thee to rise earlier, Jacob; for truth to say thou art a sluggard. Ha! good i'faith!—Let me see;—Dinner—oh! Hast thou prepared the fare I order'd yester-night?

Cook. All kill'd, and ready: but will not Sir Edward Mortimer pall on his diet? 'Tis the very same bill of fare we serv'd yesterday.

Wint. Hey—let me see—I have settled the dinners, throughout the week, in my tables. Now, by our lady, I have mistaken, and read Thursday twice over!—Ha! ha! ha!—A pestilence upon me! Well Sir Edward, (heaven bless him!) must bear with me. He must e'en dine to day on what he dined on yesterday!—'tis too late to be changed. Get thee gone, knave, get thee gone!

Cook. (*Going out.*—Age has so overdone this old Dry-bones, he'll shortly tumble from the spit.—
" Thursday

"Thurſday twice over!"—This comes of being able to read. An old buzzard! ·   (*Exit.*

Wint. Theſe fatigues of office ſomewhat wear a man. I have had a long leaſe on't. I ha' ſeen out Queen Mary, Queen Elizabeth, and King James. 'Tis e'en almoſt time that I ſhould retire, to begin to enjoy myſelf. Eh! by St. Thomas! hither trips the fair miſtreſs Blanch. Of all the waiting gentlewomen I ever looked on, during the two laſt reigns, none ſtir'd my fancy like this little roſe-bud,

Enter BLANCH.

Blanch. A good day, good Adam Winterton.

Wint. What wag! what tulip! I never ſee thee but I am a ſcore of years the younger.

Blanch. Nay, then, let us not meet often, or you will ſoon be in your ſecond child-hood.

Wint. What you come from your miſtreſs, the Lady Helen, in the foreſt here; and would ſpeak with Sir Edward Mortimer, I warrant?

Blanch. I would. Is his melancholy worſhip ſtirring yet?

Wint. Fie, you mad-cap! He is my maſter, and your Lady's Friend.

Blanch. Yes, truly, it ſeems, her only one, poor Lady: he protects her now ſhe is left an orphan.

Wint. A bleſſing on his heart! I would it were merrier. Well, ſhe is much beholden to Sir Edward for his conſolation: and he never affords her his advice but his bounty is ſure to follow it.

Blanch. Juſt ſo a crow will nouriſh its neſtling; he croaks firſt, and then gives her food.

Wint. Ha, ha! good i'faith!—but wicked, Thy company will corrupt, and lead me aſtray.

Should

Should they happen to marry, (and I have my fancies on't) I'll dance a galliard with thee, in the hall, on the round Oak table. Sbud! when I was a youth, I would ha' caper'd with St. Vitus, and beat him.

Blanch. You are as likely to dance, now, as they to marry. What has hindered them, if the parties be agreed?—yet I have, now, been with my miſtreſs theſe two years; ſince Sir Edward firſt came hither, and placed her in the cottage, hard by his lodge.

Wint. Tuſh! family reaſons.—Thou knoweſt nothing: thou art ſcarce catch'd. Two years back, when we came from Kent, and Sir Edward firſt entered on his office, here, of Head Keeper, thou wert a Colt, running wild about New Foreſt. I hired you myſelf, to attend on madam Helen.

Blanch. Nay I ſhall never forget it. But you were as frolickſome, then, as I, methinks. Doſt remember the box on the ear I gave thee, Adam?

Wint. Peace, peace, yoo pie! an you prate thus I'll ſtop your mouth. I will, by St. Thomas!

Blanch. An I be inclined to the contrary, I do not think you are able to ſtop it.

Wint. Out, you baggage! thou haſt more tricks than a kitten. Well, go thy ways. Sir Edward is at his ſtudy, and there thou wilt find him. Ah, miſtreſs Blanch! had you but ſeen me in the early part of Queen Elizabeth's reign!

Blanch. How old art thou now, Adam?

Wint. Four ſcore, come Martlemas: and, by our Lady, I can run with a lapwing.

Blanch. Canſt thou?—Well ſaid!—Thou art a merry old man, and ſhalt have a kiſs of me, on one condition.

Wint. Shall I! odſbud, name it, and 'tis mine.

Blanch.

Blanch. Then, catch me. (*Runs off.*)

Wit. Pestilence 'ont! there was a time when my legs had serv'd:—but, to speak truth, I never thrust them, now, into my scarlet hose that they do not remember me of two sticks of red sealing-wax. I was a clean limb'd stripling, when I first stood behind Sir Marmaduke's arm chair, in the old Oak eating-room.

SONG. *Adam Winterton.*

SIR Marmaduke was a hearty Knight;
    Good man! Old man!
He's painted standing bolt upright,
    With his hose roll'd over his knee;—
His Perriwig's as white as chalk;
And on his fist he holds a Hawk;
    And he looks like the head
    Of an ancient family.

II.

His dining room was long and wide;
    Good man! Old man!
His Spaniels lay by the fire-side!—
    And in other parts, d'ye see,
Cross-bows, tobacco-pipes, old hats,
A saddle, his wife, and a litter of cats;
    And he look'd like the head
    Of an ancient family.

III.

He never turn'd the poor from his gate;
    Good man! Old man!
But always ready to break the pate
    Of his Country's enemy.
What Knight could do a better thing,
Than serve the poor, and fight for his King.
    And so may every head
    Of an ancient family.

Enter WILFORD.

Wilf. Every new act of Sir Edward's charity sets me a thinking; and the more I think the more
                   I am

I am puzzled. 'Tis ſtrange that a man ſhould be ſo ill at eaſe, who is continually doing good. At times, the wild glare of his eye is frightful; and, laſt night, when I was writing for him, in the library, I could not help fancying I was ſhut up with the devil. I would ſtake my life there's a ſecret; and I could almoſt give my life to un-ravel it. I muſt to him, for my morning's employment. *(Croſſing the ſtage.)*

Wint. Ah! boy! Wilford! ſecretary! whither away, lad?

Wilf. Mr. Winterton!—Ayè, marry, this good old man has the clue, could I but coax him to give it to me.—A good morning to you, Sir!

Wint. Yea, and the like to thee, boy. Come, thou ſhalt have a cup of Canary, from my corner cup-board, yonder.

Wilf. Not a drop.

Wint. Troth, I bear thee a good will for thy honeſt, old, dead father's ſake.

Wilf. I do thankfully perceive it, Sir. Your placing me in Sir Edward's family, ſome nine months ago, when my poor father died, and left me friendleſs, will never out of my memory.

Wint. Tut, boy, no merit of mine in aſſiſting the friendleſs. 'Tis our duty child. I could never abide to ſee honeſt induſtry chop fallen. I love to have folks merry about me, to my heart.

Wilf. I would you could inſtill ſome mirth into our good maſter Sir Edward. You are an old domeſtick—the only one he brought with him, two years back, from Kent,—and might venture to give his ſpirits a jog. He ſeems devour'd with ſpleen, and melancholy.

Wint. You are a prying boy.—Go to.—I have told thee, a ſcore of times, I would not have thee

D curious

curious about our worthy mafter's humour. By
my troth, I am angry with thee. What a boy like
you?——a——Thou haft put me in choler. Con-
tinue this, and I'll undo thee;—I'll un——fbud!
I'll unproteft thee.—Ha, good i'faith! Nay,
marry, my rage holds not long:—flafh and out
again. Unproteft thee!—ha! 'twas exceeding
good, by Saint Thomas!

Wilf. I fhould ceafe to pry, fir, would you
but once, (as I think you have more than once
feem'd inclined) gratify my much-raifed curiofity.

Wint. Well faid, 'ifaith! I do not doubt thee.
I warrant thou wouldft ceafe to inquire, when I
had told thee all thou wouldft know.—What,
green-horn, didft think to trap the old man?—
Go thy ways, boy! I have a head.—Old Adam
Winterton can fift a fubtle fpeech to the bottom.

Wilf. Ah, good fir, you need not tell me that.
Young as I am, I can admire that experience,
in another, which I want myfelf.

Wint. There is fomething marvellous engag-
ing in this young man! You have a world of
promife, boy. Sixty years ago, in Queen Elizabeth's time, I was juft fuch another. I remember Marian Potpan, the farmer's daughter, of
Stocks Green, was then enamour'd of me. Well,
beware how you offend Sir Edward.

Wilf. I would not, willingly, for the world.
He has been the kindeft mafter to me. He has
inform'd my mind, relieved my diftreffes, cloath'd
me, fhelter'd me:—but, whilft my fortunes ripen
in the warmth of his goodnefs, the frozen gloom
of his countenance chills me.

Wint. Well, well, take heed how you prate
on't. Out on thefe babbling boys! There is no
keeping a fecret with younkers in a family.

Wilf.

Wilf. (*very eagerly.*) What then there *is* a secret!——'Tis as I gueffed after all.

Mint. Why, how now, hot-head?——Mercy on me! an this tinder-box boy do not make me ſhake with apprehenſion. Is it thus you take my frequent conncil?

Wilf. Dear ſir, 'tis your council which moſt I covet. Give me but that; admit me to your confidence; ſteer me with your advice, which I ever held excellent, and, with ſuch a pilot, I may ſail profperouſly through a current which, otherwiſe, might wreck me.

Wint. 'Tis melting to ſee how unfledged youth will ſhelter itſelf, like a chicken, under the wing of ſuch a tough old cock as myſelf! Well, well, I'll think on't, boy.

Wilf. The old anſwer.—Yet, he foftens apace: could I but clench him now—Faith, ſir, 'tis a raw morning; and I care not if I taſte the canary your kindneſs offer'd.

Wint. Aha! lad! ſay'ſt thou ſo? Juſt my modeſt humour when I was young. I ever refuſed my glafs at firſt, but I came to it ere I had quitted my company. Here's the key of the corner cup-board, yonder. See you do not crack the bottle, you heedleſs gooſe, you!

(*Wilford takes out the bottle and glaſſes.*)

Ha! fill it up. Od! it fparkles curiouſly. Here's to———— I prithee, tell me now, Wilford; didſt ever in thy life ſee a waiting-gentlewoman with a more inviting eye than the little Mrs. Blanch?

Wilf. Here's Mrs. Blanch—(*drinks.*)

Wint. Ah, wag! well, go thy ways! Well, when I was of thy age ————odſbud! no matter

D 2

ter; 'tis paft, now;—but here's the little Mrs.
Blanch. (drinks.)

Wilf. 'Tis thought, here, Sir Edward means to
marry her lady, Madam Helen.

Wint. Nay, I know not. She has long been
enamour'd of him, poor lady! when he was the
gay, the gallant fir Edward, in Kent. Ah, well!
two years make a wond'rous change!

Wilf. Yes, 'tis a good tough love, now a
days, that will hold out a couple of twelve-
months.

Wint. Away, I mean not fo, you giddy pate!
He is all honour; and as fteady in his courfe as
the fun: yet I wonder, fometimes, he can bear to
look upon her.

Wilf. Eh? why fo? Did not he bring her,
under his protection, to the Foreft; fince, 'tis
faid, fhe loft her relations?

Wint. Hufh, boy! on your life do not name
her uncle—I would fay her relations.

Wilf. Her uncle! wherefore? Where's the
harm in having an uncle, dead or alive?

Wint. Peace, peace! In that uncle lyes the
fecret.

Wilf. Indeed! how good Adam Winterton?
I prithee, how?

Wint. Ah! 'twas a heavy day! Poor fir Edward is now a broken fpirit—but if ever a good
fpirit walk'd the earth, in trunk hofe, he is one.

Wilf. Let us drink Sir Edward's health.

Wint. That I would, tho' 'twere a mile to the
bottom—(drinks). Ha, 'tis cheering, i'faith!
Well, in troth, I have regard for thee, boy, for
y father's fake.

Wilf. Oh, good fir! and this uncle, you fay—

Wint.

Wint. Of Madam Helen—ah!—there lyes the mifchief.

Wilf. What mifchief can be in him? why, he is dead.

Wint. Come nearer—fee you prate not now, on your life. Our good mafter, Sir Edward, was arraign'd on his account, in open court.

Wilf. Arraign'd! how mean you?

Wint. Alas, boy! tried.—Tried for ———— nearer yet—his murder.

Wilf. Mu—mur—Murder! *(drops the glafs.)*

Wint. Why, what! why, Wilford! out, alas! the boy's paffion will betray all! what, Wilford, I fay!

Wilf. You have curdled my blood!

Wint. What, varlet, thou dareft not think ill of our worthy mafter?

Wilf. I—I am his fecretary. Often alone with him at dead midnight, in his library. The candles in the fockets—and a man glaring upon me who has committed mur—ugh!

Wint. Committed! Thou art a bafe, lying knave, to fay it: and while I wear a rapier, I'll ————tufh! Heaven help me! I forget I am fourfcore. Well, well—hear me, pettifh boy, hear me. Why, look now, thou doft not attend.

Wilf. I—I mark; I mark.

Wint. I tell thee, then, our good Sir Edward was beloved in Kent; where he had returned a year before, from his travels. Madam Helen's uncle was hated by all the neighbourhood, rich and poor. A mere brute, doft mark me.

Wilf. Like enough: but when brutes walk upon two legs, the law of the land, thank Heaven! will not fuffer us to butcher them.

Wint.

Wint. Go to, you fire-brand! Our good master labour'd all he could, for many a month, to sooth his turbulence; but in vain. He pick'd a quarrel with Sir Edward, in the publick county assembly; nay, the strong ruffian struck him down, and trampled on him. Think on that, Wilford! on our good master Sir Edward, whose great soul was nigh to burst with the indignity.

Wilf. Well, but the end on't?

Wint. Why, our young master took horse, for his own house, determined, as it appear'd, to send a challenge to this white-liver'd giant, in the morning.

Wilf. I see. He kill'd him in a duel. That's another kind of butchery, which the law allows not; true humanity shudders at; and false honour justifies.

Wint. See, now, how you fly off! Sir Edward's revenge, boy, was baffled. For his antagonist was found dead in the street, that night; killed, by some unknown assassins, on his return from the assembly.

Wilf. Indeed! *unknown* assassins!

Wint. Nay, 'tis plain, our good Sir Edward had no hand in the wicked act: for he was tried, as I told you, at the next assize. Mercy on me! 'twas a crouded court; and how gentle and simple threw up their caps, at his acquittal! Heaven be thank'd! he was cleared, beyond a shadow of doubt.

Wilf. He was; I breathe again. 'Twas a happy thing. 'Twas the only way left of cleansing him from a foul suspicion.

Wint. Out alas! lad, 'tis his principal grief. He is full of nice feeling, and high-flown honour:

and

and the thought of being tried, for such a crime, has given him his heart's wound. Poor gentleman! he has shun'd the world ever since. He was once the life of all company——but now!

Sir Ed. (without) Winterton!

Wint. Hark! some one calls. Out on thee! thou has sunk my spirits into my heels. Who calls merry old Adam Winterton?

Sir Edward (without) Adam Winterton! come hither to me.

Wint. Nay, by our lady, 'tis Sir Edward himself!—Pestilence on't! if I seem sad now, 'twill be noted. I come, good Sir Edward.

" When birds—(not a word on thy life)—
    do carroll on the bush,"

" With a hey no nonny"——Mercy on me!
(Exit.

Wilf. My throat's parch'd, and my blood freezes! A quart of brandy couldn't moisten the one, nor thaw the other. This accounts, then, for all. Poor, unhappy gentleman! This unravels all, from the first day of my service—when a deep groan made me run into the library, and I found him locking up his papers, in the iron chest, as pale as ashes.—Eh?—What can be in that chest!—Perhaps some proof of——no I shudder at the suggestion.—'Tis not possible one so good can be guilty of——I know not what to think—nor what to resolve. But curiosity is roused, and, come what may, I'll have an eye upon him *(Exit.*

SCENE

SCENE III.—*A Library.*

Sir Edward Mortimer discover'd at a Writing Table. *Adam Winterton* attending:

Mort. 'Tis his first trespass, so we'll quit him,
   Adam :—
But caution him how he offend again.
As Keeper of the Forest, I should fine him.
 Wint. Nay that your worship should. He'll
   prove ere long,
—Mark but my words—a sturdy poacher. Well,
'Tis you know best.
 Mort. Well, well, no matter, Adam ;—
He has a wife, and child.
 Wint. Ah! bless your honour!
 Mort. They kill'd his dog?
 Wint. Aye, marry, sir :—a lurcher.
Black Martin Wincot the Groom Keeper shot him;
A perilous good aim.—I warrant me,
The rogue has lived this year upon that lurcher.
 Mort. Poor wretch!—Oh! well bethought;
   Send Walter to me—
I would employ him; he must ride for me,
On business of much import.
 Wint. Lackaday!
That it should chance so! I have sent him forth,
To Winchester, to buy me flannel hose;
For winter's coming on. Good lack! that things
Should fall so crossly!
 Mort. Nay, nay, do not fret—
'Tis better that my business cool, good Adam,
Than thy old limbs.
 Wint. Ah! you've a kindly heart!
 Mort. Is Wilford waiting?

           Wint.

Wint. Wilford! mercy on me!
I tremble now to hear his name. He is—
Here in the hall, fir.

   Mort. Send him in, I prithee.

   Wint. I fhall, fir. Heaven blefs you! Heaven
      blefs you!   (*Exit.*

   Mort. Good morning, good old heart! This
      honeft foul
Would feign look cheery in my houfe's gloom;
And, like a gay and fturdy ever-green,
Smiles, in the midft of blaft, and defolation,
Where all around him withers.—Well, well—
      wither!
Perifh this frail and fickle frame!—this clay,
That, in it's drofs-like compound, doth contain
The mind's pure ore, and effence.—Oh! that mind!
That mind of man! that god-like fpring of action!
That fource, whence Learning, Virtue, Honour,
      flow!—
Which lifts us to the ftars; which carries us
O'er the fwol'n waters of the angry deep,
As fwallows fkim the air.—That Fame's fole foun-
      tain!
That doth tranfmit a fair, and fpotlefs name,
When the vile trunk it rotten:—Give me that!
Oh! give me but to live, in after-age,
Remember'd and unfullied!—Heaven and earth!
Let my pure flame of Honour fhine in ftory,
When I am cold in death—and the flow fire,
That wears my vitals now, will no more move me
Than 'twould a corpfe within a monument.
    (*A knock at the door of the library.*)
   How now! Who's there? Come in.
        Enter WILFORD.
Wilford! is't you? You were not wont to knock.

   Wilf. I fear'd I might furprife you, fir.

      E   *Mort.*

Mort.   Surprife me!

Wilf.   I mean—difturb you, fir :—yes—at your
        ftudies—

Difturb you at your ftudies.

Mort.   Very ftrange!

You were not ufed to be fo cautious.

Wilf.   No—

I never ufed—but I—hum—I have learnt ——

Mort.   Learnt!

Wilf.   Better manners, fir.   I was quite raw,
When, in your bounty, you firft fhelter'd me :
But, thanks to your great goodnefs, and the leffons
Of Mr. Winterton, I ftill improve,
And pick up fomething daily.

Mort.   Aye, indeed!
Winterton !—No he dare not—Hark you, fir !
                        (ftepping up to him)

Wilf.   Sir !

Mort.   *(retreating from him).* What am I about!
        —Oh, Honour ! Honour !
Thy pile fhould be fo uniform, difplace
One atom of thee, and the flighteft breath
Of a rude peafant makes thy owner tremble
For his whole building. Reach me, from the fhelf,
The volume I was bufied in, laft night.

Wilf.   Laft night, fir ?

Mort.   Aye ;—it treats of Alexander.

Wilf.   Oh, I remember, fir—of Macedon.
I made fome extracts, by your order.   *(goes to the
                        Book-Cafe.)*

Mort.   Books
(My only commerce, now,)will fometimes roufe me.
Beyond my nature, I have been fo warm'd,
So heated by a well-turn'd rhapfody,
That I have feem'd the Hero of the tale,
So glowingly defcribed. Draw me a man
                        Struggling

Struggling for Fame, attaining, keeping it,
Dead ages since, and the Hiftorian
Decking his memory, in polifh'd phrafe,
And I can follow him through every turn,
Grow wild in his exploits, myfelf himfelf,
Until the thick pulfation of my heart
Wakes me, to ponder on the thing I am.

 Wilf. (*giving him the book*)
To my poor thinking, Sir, this Alexander
Would fcarcely roufe a man to follow him.

 Mort. Indeed! why fo lad? He is reckon'd
   brave,
Wife, generous, learn'd, by older heads than
   thine.

 Wilf. I cannot tell, fir:—I have but a glean-
   ing.—
He conquer'd all the world;—but left uncon-
   quer'd
A world of his own paffions—and they led him,
(It feems fo there) on petty provocation,
Even to murder. (*Mortimer ftarts—Wilford and*
   he exchange looks—both confufed)
I have touch'd the ftring—
'Twas unawares—I cannot help it.   (*afide*)

 Mort. (*attempting to recover himfelf.*) Wilford
——Wilford I——you miftake the character——
I, mark you—he—death and eternal tortures!
(*dafhes the book on the floor, and feizes Wilford*)
Slave! I will crufh thee! pulverife thy frame!
That no vile particle of prying nature
May——Ha, ha ha!—I will not harm thee,
   boy—
O, agony!   (*Exit.*

 Wilf. Is this the high-flown honour, and delicate feeling, old Winterton talk'd of, that cannot bear a glance at the trial?—Delicate! had I

              been

been born under a throttling planet, I had never
survived this collaring. This may be guilt. If
so——well, what have I to do with the knowledge
on't!—what *could* I do? cut off my benefactor!
who gives me bread! who is respected for his virtues, pitied for his misfortunes, loved by his family, bless'd by the poor!—Pooh! he is innocent.
This is his pride and shame. He was acquitted—
Thousands witness'd it—thousands rejoiced at it
—thousands—eh? the key left in the iron chest!
Circumstance and mystery tempt me at every
turn. Ought I—no matter. These are no com-
mon incitements, and I submit to the impulse. I
heard him stride down the stairs. It opens with a
spring I see. I tremble in every joint *(goes to the
chest.*

Enter Sir EDWARD MORTIMER

Mort. I had forgot the key and——ha! by
    hell!

(*Sees* Wilford ; *snatches a pistol from the table, runs
up to him, and holds it to his head. Wilford on
his knees, claps down the lid of the trunk which he
has just open'd. After an apparent struggle of
mind,* Mortimer *throws the pistol from him.*)

Mort. Begone !——Come back.—Come hi-
    ther to me.

Mark me—I see thou dost at every turn—
And I have noted thee too. Thou hast found
(I know not how) some clue to my disgrace :—
Aye, my disgrace—we must not mince it now—
Publick dishonour !—trod on !—buffeted !
Then tried as the foul demon who had foil'd
My manly means of vengeance. Anguish gnaws
    me :
Mountains of shame are piled upon me !—Me,
                   Who

Who have made Fame my idol. 'Twas enough!
But fomething muft be fuper-added : You,—
A worm, a viper I have warm'd, muft plant,
In venom'd fport, your fting into my wounds,
Too tender e'en for tendernefs to touch,
And work me into madnefs. Thou wouldft
            queftion
My very——flave!——my very innocence ;
Ne'er doubted yet by judges nor arraigners.
Wretch! you have wrung this from me. Be
            content,
I am funk low enough.
    Wilf. (*returning the key*) Oh, fir! I ever
Honour'd and loved you. But I merit all.
My paffions hurried me I know not whither.
Do with me as you pleafe, my kind, wrong'd
            mafter !
Difcard me—thruft me forth—nay, kill me!——
    Mort. Kill you !
    Wilf. I know not what I fay.—I know but this,
That I would die to ferve you.

Enter a Servant.

    Serv. Sir, your brother.
Is juft alighted at the gate.
    Mort. My brother !
He could not time it worfe. Wilford, remember!
Come fhew me to him.   (*Exit with fervant.*
    Wilf. Remember! I fhall never while I live
forget it: nay, I fhall never, while I live, forgive
myfelf. My knees knock together ftill; and the
cold drops ftand on my forehead, like rain-water
on a pent-houfe.

Enter BARBARA.

    Barbara. Wilford !

Wilf.

Wilf. Eh? Barbara! How cameſt thou here?

Barb. With my father, who waits below, to ſee Sir Edward.

Wilf. He————He is buſied; he cannot ſee him now. He is with his brother.

Barb. Troth, I am ſorry for it. My poor father's heart is burſting with gratitude, and he would fain eaſe it, by pouring out his thanks to his benefactor. Oh, Wilford, your's is a happy lot to have ſuch a maſter as Sir Edward!

Wilf. Happy? Oh! yes—I—I am very happy.

Barb. Mercy! has any ill befallen you?

Wilf. No; nothing. 'Tis all my happineſs. My happineſs is like your father's gratitude, Barbara; and, at times, it goes near to choak me.

Barb. Nay, I'm ſure there's more in this. Bleſs me, you look pale! I cou'dn't bear to ſee you ill, or uneaſy, Wilford.

Wilf. Cou'dn't you, Barbara? Well, well, I ſhall be better preſently. 'Tis nothing of import.

Barb. Truſt me, I hope not.

Wilf. Well, queſtion me no more on't now, I beſeech you, Barbara.

Barb. Believe me, I would not queſtion you but to conſole you, Wilford. I would ſcorn to pry into any one's grief; much more your's, Wilford, to ſatisfy a buſy curioſity. Though, I am told, there are ſuch in the world who would.

Wilf. I————I am afraid there are, Barbara. But come, no more of this. 'Tis a paſſing cloud on my ſpirits, and will ſoon blow over,

Barb. Ah! could I govern your fortunes, foul weather ſhould ne'er harm you.

Wilf. Should not it, ſweet! Kiſs me. (*Kiſſes her.*) The lips of a woman are a ſovereign cordial for melancholy.

DUET.

DUET.

WILFORD AND BARBARA.

Wilf. Sweet little Barbara, when you are advancing,
Sweet little Barbara, my cares you remove;
Barb. Poor little Barbara can feel her heart dancing,
When little Barbara is met by her love.
Wilf. When I am grieved, love! oh, what would you say?
Barb.　　Tattle to you, love,
　　And prattle to you, love,
And laugh your grief and care away.
Wilf.　　Sweet little Barbara, &c.
Barb.　　Poor little Barbara, &c.

Wilf. Yet, dearest Barbara, look all through the nation,
Care, soon or late, my love, is ev'ry man's lot.
Barb. Sorrow and melancholy, grief and vexation,
When we are young and jolly, soon is forgot.
Wilf. When we grow old, love! then what will you say?
Barb.　　Tattle to you, love,
　　And prattle to you, love,
And laugh your grief and care away.
Wilf.　　Sweet little Barbara, &c.
Barb.　　Poor little Barbara, &c.

END OF THE FIRST ACT.

ACT

ACT II.

SCENE I.—*The New Forest.*

Enter ARMSTRONG *and* ORSON.

Arm. GO to—I tell thee Orson, (as I have told thee more than once) thou art too sanguinary.

Orf. And, I tell you, Captain Armstrong—but always under favour, you being our leader—you are too humane.

Arm. Humanity is scarcely counted a fault: if so, 'tis a fault on the right side.

Orf. Umph! perhaps not with us. We are robbers.

Arm. And why should robbers lack humanity? They who plunder most respect it as a virtue, and make a shew on't, to guild their vices. Lawyers, Physicians, Placemen, all——all plunder and slay, but all pretend to humanity.

Orf. They are Regulars, and plunder by licence.

Arm. Then let us Quacks set the Regulars a better example.

Orf. This humanity, Captain, is a high horse you are ever bestride upon. Some day, mark my word, he'll fling you.

Arm.

Arm. Cruelty is a more dangerous beaſt :——
When the rider's thrown, his brains are kick'd
out, and no one pities him.

Orſ. Like enough;——but your tough horſe-
man, who ventures boldly, is never diſmounted.
When I am engaged in a deſperate chace, (as we
are, Captain,) I ſtick at nothing. I hate milk
ſops.

Arm. And love mutiny. Take heed, Orſon;
I have before caution'd you not to glance at me.

Orſ. I ſay nothing : but if ſome eſcape to inform againſt us, whom we have rob'd, 'tis none
of my fault. Dead men tell no tales.

Arm. Wretch! Speak that again, and you
ſhall tell none. (*holds a carbine to his head.*)

Orſ. Flaſh away!——I don't fear death.

Arm. More ſhame for thee; for thou art unfit
to meet it.

Orſ. I know my trade. I ſet powder, ball,
and rope, at defiance.

Arm. Brute! You miſtake headſtrong inſen-
ſibility for courage. Do not miſtake my horror of
it for cowardice : for I, who ſhudder at cruelty,
will fell your boldneſs to the earth, when I ſee you
practice it. Submit.

Orſ I do. I know not what 'tis, but I have
told you, often, there is ſomething about you
awes me. I cannot tell——I could kill twenty to
your one.

Arm. There 'tis.——Thou wouldſt dart upon
weak unguarded man, like a tyger. A ferocious
animal, whether crawling or erect, ever ſhrinks
from fair oppoſition.

Orſ. My courage was never yet doubted, Captain.

F   *Arm.*

Arm. Your nerves, fool. Thou art a mere
machine. Could I but give it motion, I would
take an oak from the foreſt, here, clap a flint into
it for heart, and make as bold a fellow as thou art.
Liſten to my orders.

Orſ. I obey.

Arm. Get thee to our den. Put on thy diſ-
guiſe—then hie thee to the market town for proviſion, for our company. Here——Here is part
of the ſpoil we took yeſter-night : ſee you bring
an honeſt account of what you lay out. *(giving
money)*

Orſ. My honour!——

Arm. Well, I do not doubt thee, here. Our
profeſſion is ſingular; it's followers do not cheat
one another. You will not be back till duſk. See
you fall not on any poor ſtraggling peaſant, as you
return.

Orſ. I would feign encounter the ſolitary man,
who is ſometimes wandering by night about the
foreſt. He is rich.

Arm. Not for your life. 'Tis Sir Edward,
Mortimer, the head Keeper. Touch him not;
'tis too near home. Beſides, he is no object for
plunder. I have watch'd him, at midnight, ſteal-
ing from his lodge, to wander like one crazed.
He is good, too, to the poor; and ſhould walk
unmoleſted by Charity's charter. 'Twere pity that
he who adminiſters to neceſſity, all day, ſhould be
rifled by neceſſity at night. An thou ſhouldſt
meet him, I charge thee ſpare him.

Orſ. I muſt, if it be your order. This ſparing
doctrine will go nigh, at laſt, to ſtarve all the
thieves. When a man takes to the trade of a wolf,
he ſhould not go like a lamb to his buſineſs. *(Exit*
                                                    Arm.

Arm. This fellow is downright villain: Harden'd and relentless. I have felt, in my penury, the world trample on me. It has driven me to take that, desperately, which wanting I should starve. Death! my spirit cannot brook to see a sleek knave walk negligently by his fellow in misery, and suffer him to rot. I will wrench that comfort from him which he will not bestow.—But nature puts a bar:—Let him administer to my wants, and pass on:—I have done with him.

SONG.

Armstrong.

When the Robber his victim has noted,
    When the Free-booter darts on his prey,
Let Humanity spare the devoted;
    Let Mercy forbid him to slay.

Since my hope is by penury blighted,
    My sword must the traveller daunt;
I will snatch from the rich man, benighted,
    The gold he denies to my want.

But the victim when, once, I have noted,
    At my foot when I look on my prey,
Let Humanity spare the devoted;
    Let Mercy forbid me to slay.

SCENE II. *The Hall in* Sir EDWARD MORTIMER'S *Lodge.*

Enter FITZHARDING.

Fitz. Well, business must be minded:—but he stays
A tedious time, methinks.—You fellow!
        (*To a Servant crossing the hall.*

Serv. Sir!

Fitz.

Fitz Where is Sir Triftful? Where's Don Me-
    lancholy?

Serv. Who, fir?

Fitz. My brother, knave, Sir Edward Mor-
    timer.

Serv. He was with you, but now, Sir.

Fitz. Sir, I thank you ;—

That's information. Louts, and ferving-men,
Can never parley ftraight. I met a fellow,
Here, on my way acrofs the heath,—a Hind—
And afk'd how far to Lymington : I look'd
The anfwer would have bolted from his chops,
Bounce, like a pellet from a popgun.—No :—
He ftared, and fcratch'd his empty head, and cried,
" Where do you come from?"———Who brought
    in my luggage?

Serv It was not I, fir.

Fitz. There!—They never can!

Go to your mafter; pray him to defpatch
His houfhould work :—tell him I hate fat Folios.
Plague ! when I crofs the country, here, to fee
    him,
He leaves me, ram'd into an elbow chair,
With a huge, heavy book, that makes me nod,
Then tumbles on my toes. Tell him, do'ft hear,
Captain Fitharding's company has tired me.

Serv. Who's company ?——

Fitz. My own, knave.

Serv. Sir, I fhall.   *(Exit.*

Fitz. A book to me's a fovereign Narcotick;
A lump of opium; every line a dofe.
Edward is all deep reading, and black letter;
He fhews it in his very chin. He fpeaks
Mere Dictionary; and he pores on pages
That give plain men the head-ache. " Scarce,
    and curious,"

                        Are

Are baits his learning nibbles at.   His brain
Is cram'd with mouldy volumes, cramp, and ufe-
　　lefs,
Like a librarian's lumber-room.—Poor fellow!
Grief will do much!—well! fome it drives to
　　reading,
And fome to drinking:—'twill do much!—this
　　trial——
A fool to fret fo for't! his honour's clear.
Tut! I'm a foldier—know what honour is.
Had I been flander'd, and a fair Court martial
Cleanfed me from calumny, as white as fnow,
I had ne'er moped, and fumed, and winced, and
　　kick'd,
But fat down heart-whole. Plague upon't! this
　　houfe
Appears the very cave of melancholy.
Nay, hold, I lie:—here comes a petticoat.
Enter BLANCH.
Od! a rare wench! This is the beft edition
In Edward's whole collection. Here, come hither!
Let me perufe you.
　　Blanch. Would you fpeak to me, Sir?
　　Fizt. Aye, child. I'm going now to read you.
　　Blanch. Read me!
You'll find me full of errors, fir.
　　Fitz No matter.
Come nearer, child: I cannot fee to read
At fuch a diftance.
　　Blanch. You had better, Sir,
Put on your fpectacles.
　　Fitz. Aye, there fhe has me!
A plague upon old Time! old Scythe and Hour-
　　glafs
Has fet his mark upon me. Harkye, child:
You do not know me. You and I muft have
Better

Better acquaintance.

  Blanch. O, I've heard of you.
You are Sir Edward's kinfman, Sir—his brother.

  Fitz. Aye—his half brother—by the mother's
    fide—
His elder brother.

  Blanch. Yes, Sir, I fee that.

  Fitz. This gypfey's tongue is like her eye: I
    know not
Which is the fharpeft.   Tell me what's your
    name.

  Blanch. My name is Blanch, Sir—born, here,
    in the foreft.

  Fitz. Sbud! I muft be a Keeper in this foreft.
Whither art going, fweet one?

  Blanch. Home, Sir.

  Fitz. Home!
Why is not this thy home?

  Blanch. No, Sir; I live
Some half mile hence—with madam Helen, Sir.
I brought a letter from her, to Sir Edward.

  Fitz. Odfo, with Helen!—fo—with her!—the
    object
Of my grave brother's groaning paffion. Plague!
I would 'twere in the houfe.   I do not like
Your rheumatick, October affignations,
Under an elm, by moonlight. This will end
In flannels and fciatica.   My paffion
Is not Arcadian.   Tell me, pretty one,
Shall I walk with you, home?

  Blanch. No, Sir, I thank you;
It would fatigue you, fadly.

  Fitz. Fatigue me!
Oons! this wild foreft filly, here, would make me
Grandfather to Methufaleh.   Look here—
Here is a purfe of money.

Blanch.

Blanch. O, the father!
What will you give me any?

Fitz. Gold I find
The univerfal key; the *paffe par tout.*
It will unlock a foreft maiden's heart,
As eafy as a politician's.   Here;
Here are two pieces, rofe-bud.   Buy a top-knot;
Make thyfelf happy with them.

Blanch. That I will.
The poor old woman, northward of the lodge,
Lyes fick in bed.   I'll take her this, poor foul,
To comfort her.

Fitz.   Hold!—hey the devil!—hold.
This was not meant to comfort an old woman.

Blanch Why, would'nt you relieve her, Sir?

Fitz. Um?——ves:—
But—pfhaw! pooh, prithee—there's a time for
    all things.
Why tell me of her now,—of an old fool,—
Of comforting the aged, now?

Blanch. I thought
That you might have a fellow feeling, Sir.

Fitz. This little paftoral devil's laughing at me!
Oons! come and kifs me, jade.   I am a Soldier,
And Juftice of the Peace.

Blanch. Then, fhame upon you!
Your double calling might have taught you better.
I fee your drift, now.   Take your dirt again,
                    (throws down the money.)
Good Captain Juftice!—Stoop for it,—and think
How an old Soldier, and a Juftice looks,
When he is picking up the bribes he offers,
To injure thofe he fhould protect;—the helplefs,
The poor, and innocent.   [*Exit.*

Fitz. I warrant me,
Could I but fee my face, now, in a glafs,

                                    That

That I look wond'rous sheepish. I'm ashamed
To pick up the two pieces.—Let them lye.—
I would not wrong the innocent;—good reason;—
There be so few that are so:—she is honest;
I must make reparation. Odso! Wilford!

Enter WILFORD.

How fares it. boy?
 Wilf. I thank you, Sir. I hope you have en-
   joy'd
Your health, these three months past, since last
   you honour'd us
With your good presence, at the lodge.
 Fitz. Indifferent.
Some cramps and shooting pains, boy. I have
   dropt
Some cash here, but I am afraid to bend
To pick it up again, lest it should give me
An aukward twinge. Stoop for it, honest Wilford.
There's a good lad!
 Wilf. Right willingly, Sir. (*Picks up the money.*)
 Fitz. So!
The Soldier and the Justice save their blushes.—
Now, carry it, I prithee, at your leisure,
To an old gossip, near the lodge here—north-
   ward—
I've heard of her—she's bed-ridden, and sick.
You need not say who sent you.
 Wilf. I conceive.
'Tis private bounty; that's true charity.
 Fitz. Nay, pish!—my charity!——
 Wilf. Nay. I could swear
'Tis not the first time you have offer'd this
In secret.
 Fitz. Um!—why no;—not quite the first.
But tell me, lad, how jogs the world here, eh?
          In

In Rueful Caftle?—What, fome three months back,
We two were cronies. What, haft thou forgot?
Thou wert my favourite here, man.

Wilf. Sir, you honour'd me
By faying fo.

Fitz. Tut! honour'd!—tut—a fig!
Thou art grown ftarch, and fad. This air is catch-
ing;
Thou art infected. Harkye, Wilford, harkye!
Thou'rt a fly rogue! What you could never tell
me
Of Helen's waiting maid; the little cherry;—
Of——plague upon her name!—of——

Wilf. Blanch, Sir ?

Fitz. Blanch:
That's it;—the foreft fairy.—You and I
Muft have fome talk about her.

Wilf. Have you feen her?

Fitz. Juft now: juft gone. Od! I have blun-
der'd horribly!
You muft know, lad——come hither.

(They retire to the back of the fcene.)

Enter SIR EDWARD MORTIMER.

Mort. Now for my brother, and—Ha! Wil-
ford with him!
That imp is made my fcourge. They whifper too!
O! I had rather court the thunder-bolt,
To melt my bones, and pound me to a mafs,
Than fuffer this vile canker to corrode me.
Wilford!

Wilf. Who calls?—eh!—'tis Sir Edward.

Fitz. Mum!

Mort. I feem to interrupt you.

Wilf. (earneftly.) No, indeed.

G No.

No, on my life, fir:—we were only talking
Of ————

 Fitz. Hold your tongue. Oons! boy, you
   muft not tell.

Mort. Not!

Fitz. Not! no to be fure:—why, 'tis a fecret.

Wilf. You fhall know all, fir.—'Twas a trifle—
   nothing—
In faith, you fhall know all.

 Fitz. In faith, you lie.
Be fatisfied, good Edward:—'tis a toy.—
But, of all men, I would not have thee know on't.
It is a tender fubject.

 Mort. Aye, indeed!

 Fitz. May not I have my fecret? Oons!
   good brother,
What would you fay, now, fhould a meddling
   knave
Bufy his brains with matters, though but trivial,
Which concern you alone?

 Mort. I'd have him rot:
Die piecemeal; pine; moulder in mifery.
Agent, and facrifice to Heaven's wrath,
When caftigating plagues are hurl'd on man,
Stands lean, and lynx-eyed Curiofity,
Watching his neighbour's foul. Sleeplefs himfelf
To banifh fleep from others. Like a Leech
Sucking the blood-drops from a care-worn heart,
He gorges on't—then renders up his food,
To nourifh Calumny, his foul-lung'd mate,
Who carries Rumour's trumpet; and whofe breath,
Infecting the wide furface of the world,
Strikes peftilence and blight. O, fie, ont! fie!
Whip me the curious wretch from pole to pole!
         Who

Who writhes in fire, and fcorches all around him,
A victim making victims!

Fitz. By the mafs,
'Twere a found whipping that, from pole to pole!
From conftable to conftable might ferve.
E'en you yourfelf were like to prove, but now,
This Leech, that's yoke-fellow, you fay, to Scan-
dal,
The bad-breath'd trumpeter.

Mort. Your pardon, brother;
I had forgot. Wilford, I've bufinefs for you.
Wait for me—aye—an hour after dinner,
Wait for me in the library.

Wilf. The library!——
I ficken at the found. (*afide.*) Wait there for you—
and—
Captain Fitzharding, Sir?

Mort. For me, alone.

Wilf. Alone, Sir!

Mort. Yes,—begone.

Wilf. I fhall, fir—but,
If I have ever breath'd a fyllable
That might difpleafe you may——

Mort. Fool! breathe no more.

Wilf. I'm dumb.
I'd rather ftep into a Lion's den
Than meet him in the library!—I go, Sir. [*Exit.*

Fitz. Brother, you are too harfh with that poor
boy.

Mort. Brother, a man muft rule his family
In his own way.

Fitz. Well, well, well—Don't be touchy.
I fpeak not to offend: I only fpeak
On a friend's privilege. The Poor are men,
And have their feelings, brother.

Mort. So have I!

Fitz.

Fitz. One of the beſt that we can ſhew, believe
   me,
Is mildneſs to a ſervant.   Servants, brother,
Are born with fortune's yoke about their necks;
And that is galling in itſelf enough;
We ſhould not goad them under it.   The maſter
Should rather cheer them in their ſervitude,
With kindly words—not too familiar neither;
But utter'd with that air which true benevolence
Imparts to dignified nobility.
 Mort. Brother, your hand.   You have a gen-
   tle nature—
May no miſchance e'er ruffle it, my brother!
I've known thee from my infancy, old ſoldier;
And never did I know—I do not flatter—
A heart more ſtout, more caſed with hardy man-
   hood,
More full of milk within.   Truſt me, dear friend,
If admiration of thy charity
May argue charity in the admirer,
I am not deſtitute.
 Fitz. You!—I have ſeen you
Sometimes o'erflow with it.
 Mort. And what avails it?
Honour has been my theme; good will to man
My ſtudy.   I have labour'd for a name
As white as mountain ſnow; dazzling, and ſpeck-
   leſs:
Shame on't! 'tis blur'd with blots! Fate, like a
   mildew,
Ruins the virtuous harveſt I would reap,
And all my crop is weeds.
 Fitz. Why, how now brother!
This is all ſpleen.   You mope yourſelf too much,
In this dull foreſt, here.   Twenty blue devils
       Are

Are dancing jigs, and hornpipes, in your brains.
Fie, fie! be more a man.

 Mort. Well I have done.

 Fitz. Come, what's for dinner? Od? I mean
   to eat
Abundantly.

 Mort. I know not, brother. Honeft Winterton
Will tell you all.

 Fitz. What he! old Adam! he!
My merry buck of Paradife?——Odfo!
I have not feen him. Well he fhall produce
A flaggon of the beft; and, after dinner,
We will be jovial. Come, come, roufe you, man!
I came on purpofe, thirty miles from home,
To jog your fpirits. Prithee, now, be gay!
And, prithee, too, be kind to my young favourite!
To Wilford there.

 Mort. Well, well; I hope I have been.

 Fitz. No doubt, in actions:——but in words,
   and looks.——
A rugged look's a damper to a greenhorn.
I watch'd him, now, when you frown'd angerly
And he betray'd——

 Mort. Betray'd!

 Fitz. Ten thoufand fears.

 Mort. Oh!

 Fitz. The poor devil couldn't fhew more
   fcared
Had you e'en held a piftol to his head.
        (Mortimer ftarts)
Why hey-day! what's the matter?

 Mort. Brother!————
Queftion me not; my nerves are afpin-like;
The flighteft breath will fhake 'em. Come, good
   brother.
           Fitz.

Fitz. You'll promiſe to be gay?

Mort. I'll do my beſt.

Fitz. Why that's well ſaid! A man can do no
more.

Od! I believe my rattling talk has given you
A ſtir already.

Mort. That it has indeed!

Come, brother!

[*Exeunt.*

SCENE III. *Helen's Cottage.*

Enter HELEN *and* SAMSON.

Helen. Are you he that wiſh to enter in my
ſervice?

Samſ. Yes, ſo pleaſe you, Madam Helen, for
want of a better.

Helen. Why, I have ſeen you in the foreſt—
at Rawbold's cottage. He is your father, as I
think.

Samſ. Yes, ſo pleaſe you, Madam; for want
of a better.

Helen. I fear me you may well ſay that. Your
father, as I have heard, bears an ill name, in the
foreſt.

Samſ. Alas! madam, he is obliged to bear it
—for want of a better. We are all famiſh'd,
madam: and the naked and hungry have ſel-
dom many friends to ſpeak well of them.

Helen. If I ſhould hire thee, who will give
thee a character?

Samſ. My father, madam.

Helen. Why ſirrah, he has none of his own.

Samſ. The more fatherly in him, madam, to
give his ſon what he has need of, for himſelf. But

a knave

a knave is often applied to, to vouch for a good
servant's honesty. I will serve you as faithfully
as your last footman; who, I have heard, ran
away this morning.

Helen. Truly, he did so.

Samf. I was told on't, some half hour ago; and
ran, hungrily, hither, to offer myself. So, please
you, let not poverty stand in the way of my preferment.

Helen. Should I entertain you, what could you
do to make yourself useful?

Samf. Any thing. I can wire hares, snare
partridges, shoot a buck, and smuggle brandy,
for you, madam.

Helen. Fie on you, knave! 'Twere fitter to
turn you over to the Verderors of the forest, for
punishment, than to encourage you in such prac-
tices.

Samf. I would practice any thing better, that
might get me bread. I would scrape trenchers,
fill buckets, and carry a message. What can a
man do! He can't starve.

Helen. Well, sirrah, to snatch thee from evil,
I care not if I make trial of thee?

Sarf. No! will you?

Helen. Nineteen in twenty might question my
prudence for this:—but, whatever loss I may suffer from thy roguery, the thought of having open'd
a path to lead a needy wanderer back to virtue
will more than repay me.

Samf. O, bless, you, lady! If I do not prove
virtuous never trust in man more. I am over-
joy'd!

Helen. Get thee to the kitchen. You will find
a livery there will suit you.

Samf.

Samf. A livery! O, the father! Virtuous and a livery, all in a few feconds! Heaven blefs you!

Helen. Well, get you to your work.

Samf. I go, madam. . If I break any think to day, befeech you let it go for nothing; for joy makes my hand tremble. Should you want me, pleafe to cry Samfon, and I am with you in a twinkling· Heaven blefs you! Here's fortune!

                         (*Exit.*

Helen. Blanch ftays a tedious time. ·Heaven fend Mortimer's health be not worfe! He is fadly altered fince we came to the foreft. I dream'd, laft night, of the fire he faved me from; and I faw him, all frefh, in manly bloom, bearing me through the flames, even as it once happened.

Enter BLANCH.

Helen. How now wench! You have almoft tired my patience.

Blanch. And my own legs, madam. If the old footman had not made fo much ufe of his, by running away, they might have fpared mine.

Henlen. Inform me of Sir Edward Mortimer. Haft feen him?

Blanch. Yes, I have, madam.

Helen. Say; tell me; How look'd he? how's his health? is he in fpirits? What faid he, Blanch? Will he be here to day?

Blanch A little breath, madam, and I will an-
       fwer all, duly.

Helen. O! fie upon thee, wench! Thefe interrogatories fhould be anfwered Quicker than breath can utter them.

Blanch. That's impoffible, lady.

                             Helen.

Helen. Thou would'ſt not ſay ſo hadſt thou ever
    loved.
Love has a fleeter meſſenger than ſpeech,
To tell love's meaning. His expreſſes poſt
Upon the orbs of viſion, ere the tongue
Can ſhape them into words. A lovers's look
Is his heart's Mercury. O! the Eye's eloquence,
Twin-born with thought, outſtrips the tardy voice,
Far ſwifter than the nimble lightning's flaſh
The ſluggiſh thunder-peal that follows it.

  Blanch. I am not ſkill'd in eye-talking, madam.
I have been uſed to let my diſcourſe ride upon my
tongue; and, I have been told, 'twill trot at a good
round pace upon occaſion.

  Helen. Then let it gallop, now, beſeech you,
    wench,
And bring me news of Mortimer.

  Blanch. Then, madam, I ſaw Sir Edward in his
library: and deliver'd your letter. He will be
here, either in the evening, or on the morrow: 'tis
uncertain which—for his brother, Captain Fitzharding, is arrived, on a viſit to him.

  Helen. Is he?—well, that may ſomewhat raiſe
    his ſpirits.
That ſoldier has a pleaſant, harmleſs mind.
Mirth gilds his age, and ſits upon his brow
Like ſun in winter. I ne'er ſaw a man
More cheerful in decline, more laughter-loving,
More gay, and frolickſome.

  Blanch. Frolickſome enough, if you knew all—
But not ſo harmleſs.   *(aſide.)*

  Helen. He'll ſcarce be here to night.

  Blanch. Who? Sir Edward? Haply not, madam;
but his letter may chance to ſpecify further parti-
culars.

           H   *Helen.*

Helen. His letter ! Has he written ?—fie upon
   thee !
Why didft not give it me, at once ? Where is it ?
Thou art turn'd dreamer, wench !—Come, quickly.

Blanch. You talk'd to me fo much of reading
eyes, madam, that I e'en forgot the letter. Here
it is.

Helen. Come to me, fhortly, in my cabinet:
I'll read it there.—I am almoft unfit
To open it   I ne'er receive his letters
But my hand trembles. Well, I know 'tis filly,
And yet I cannot help it.   I will ring ;
Then come to me, good Blanch—not yet. My
   Mortimer,
Now for your letter !   *(Exit.*

Blanch. I would they were wedded once, and
all this trembling would be over. I am told
your married lady's feelings are little roufed in
reading letters from a hufband.

Enter SAMSON—*drefs'd in a Livery.*

Sam. This fudden turn of fortune might puff
fome men up with pride. I have look'd in the
glafs already :—and if ever man look'd braver in
a glafs than I, I know nothing of finery.

Blanch. Hey day ! who have we here ?

Sam. Oh, lord ! this is the maid.——I mean
the waiting-woman.   I warrant we fhall be rare
company, in a long winter's evening.

Blanch. Why, who are you ?

Sam. I'm your fellow-fervant:—the new comer.
The laft footman caft his fkin in the pantry this
morning, and I have crept into it.

Blanch. Why, fure, it cannot be !—Now I look
upon you again, you are Samfon Rawbold—old
Rawbold's fon, of the foreft, here.

Sam.

Sam. The fame; I am not like fome upftarts; When I am profperous, I do not turn my back on my poor relations.

Blanch. What, has my lady hired thee?

Samf. She has taken me, like a pad nag, upon trial.

Blanch. I fufpect you will play her a jade's trick, and ftumble in your probation. You have been caught tripping, ere now.

Samf. An I do not give content 'tis none of my fault. A man's qualities cannot come out all at once. I wifh you would teach me a little how to lay a cloth.

Blanch. You are well qualified for your office, truly, not to know that.

Samf. To fay truth, we had little practice that way, at home. We ftood not upon forms. We had fometimes no cloth for a dinner——

Blanch. And, fometimes, no dinner for a cloth.

Samf. Juft fo. We had little order in our family.

Blanch. Well, I will inftruct you.

Samf. That's kind. I will be grateful. They tell me I have learnt nothing but wickednefs, yet: but I will inftruct you in any thing I know, in return.

Blanch. There I have no mind to become your fcholar. But be fteady in your fervice, and you may outlive your beggary, and grow into refpect.

Samf. Nay, an riches rain upon me, refpect will grow of courfe. I never knew a rich man yet who wanted followers to pull off their caps to him.

SONG.

SAMSON.

I.

A traveller ſtopt at a widow's gate;
She kept an Inn, and he wanted to bait;——
  But the landlady ſlighted her gueſt:
For when Nature was making an ugly race,
She certainly moulded the traveller's face
  As a ſample for all the reſt.

II.

The chamber-maid's ſides they were ready to crack,
When ſhe ſaw his queer noſe, and the hump at his back;--
  A hump is'nt handſome, no doubt——
And, though 'tis confeſs'd that the prejudice goes,
Very ſtrongly, in favour of wearing a noſe,
  Yet a noſe ſhould'nt look like a ſnout.

III.

A bag full of gold on the table he laid——
'Thad a wond'rous effect on the widow and maid!
  And they quickly grew marvellous civil.
The money immediately alter'd the caſe;
They were charm'd with his hump, and his ſnout, and his face,
  Tho' he ſtill might have frighten'd the devil.

IV.

He paid like a prince—gave the widow a ſmack——
Then flop'd on his horſe, at the door, like a ſack;
  While the landlady, touching the chink,
Cried---" Sir, ſhould you travel this country again,
" I heartily hope that the ſweeteſt of men
  " Will ſtop at the widow's to drink."

Exeunt.

SCENE

SCENE IV: *The* LIBRARY.

WILFORD, *discovered.*

Wilf. I would Sir Edward were come! The dread of a fearful encounter is, often, as terrible as the encounter itself. Yet my encounters with him, of late, are no trifles. Some few hours back, in this very room, he held a loaded pistol within an inch of my brains. Well, that was passion—he threw it from him on the instant, and—eh!— He's coming.—No. The old wainscot cracks and frightens me out of my wits: and, I verily believe, the great folio dropt on my head, just now, from the shelf, on purpose to increase my terrors.

(*Enter* Sir EDWARD MORTIMER, *at one door of the Library, which he locks after him.* WILFORD *turns round on hearing him shut it.*)

Wilf. What's that ?—'Tis he himself! Mercy on me! he has lock'd the door!—What is going to become of me!

Mort. Wilford!—Is no one in the picture gallery ?

Wilf. No——not a soul, Sir——Not a human soul—
None within hearing, if I were to bawl
Ever so loud.

Mort. Lock yonder door.

Wilf. The door, Sir!

Mort. Do as I bid you.

Wilf. What, si ? Lock—— (*Mortimer waves with his hand.*)
I shall, Sir, (*going to the door and locking it.*)

His

His face has little anger in it, neither:
'Tis rather mark'd with forrow, and diftrefs.

 Mort. Wilford approach me.——What am I to fay
For aiming at your life!——Do you not fcorn me,
Defpife me for it?

 Wilf. I! Oh, Sir!————

 Mort. You muft.
For I am fingled from the herd of men,
A vile, heart-broken wretch!

 Wilf. Indeed, indeed, Sir,
You deeply wrong yourfelf. Your equal's love,
The poor man's prayer, the orphan's tear of gra-
   titude,
All follow you:——and I!——I owe you all!
I am moft bound to blefs you.

 Mort. Mark me, Wilford.——
I know the value of the orphan's tear,
The poor man's prayer, refpect from the refpected;
I feel to merit thefe, and to obtain them,
Is to tafte here, below, that thrilling cordial
Which the remunerating Angel draws,
From the eternal fountain of delight,
To pour on bleffed fouls, that enter heaven.
I feel this:——I!——How muft my nature, then,
Revolt at him who feeks to ftain his hand,
In human blood?——and yet it feems, this day,
I fought your life.——O! I have fuffer'd madnefs——
None know my tortures——pangs!——but I can end
  · them:
End them as far as appertains to thee.——
I have refolv'd it.——Hell born ftruggles tear me!
But I have ponder'd on't,——and I muft truft thee.

 Wilf. Your confidence fhall not be ————

 Mort. You muft fwear.

 Wilf. Swear, Sir!——will nothing but an oath,
  then ————

         Mort.

Mort. Liften.

May all the ills that wait on frail humanity
Be doubled on your head, if you difclofe
My fatal fecret! May your body turn
Moft lazar-like, and loathfome; and your mind
More loathfome than your body! May thofe fiends
Who ftrangle babes, for very wantonnefs,
Shrink back, and fhudder at your monftrous crimes,
And, fhrinking, curfe you! Palfies ftrike your
      youth!
And the fharp terrors of a guilty mind
Poifon your aged days; while all your nights,
As on the earth you lay your houfelefs head,
Out-horror horror! May you quit the world
Abhor'd, felf-hated, hopelefs for the next,
Your life a burthen, and your death a fear!

    Wilf. For mercy's fake, forbear! you terrify
      me!

    Mort. Hope this may fall upon thee;—Swear
      thou hopeft it,
By every attribute which heaven, earth, hell,
Can lend, to bind, and ftrengthen conjuration,
If thou betray'ft me.

    Wilf. Well I —— (*hefitating.*)

    Mort. No retreating!

    Wilf. (*after a paufe.*)
I fwear by all the ties that bind a man,
Divine, or human,—never to divulge!

    Mort. Remember you have fought this fecret:
      —Yes,
Extorted it. I have not thruft it on you.
'Tis big with danger to you; and to me,
While I prepare to fpeak, torment unutterable.
Know, Wilford that —— damnation!

    Wilf. Deareft Sir!
Collect yourfelf. This fhakes you horribly.

                     You

You had this trembling, it is scarce a week,
At Madam Helen's.

    Mort. There it is.—Her uncle—

    Wilf. Her uncle!

    Mort. Him. She knows it not—None know
          it—

You are the first ordain'd to hear me say,
I am——his murderer.

    Wilf. O, heaven!

    Mort. His assassin.

    Wilf. What you that—mur—the murder—
          I am choak'd!

    Mort. Honour, thou blood-stain'd God! at
          whose red altar

Sit War and Homicide, O, to what madness
Will insult drive thy votaries! By heaven,
In the world's range there does not breathe a man
Whose brutal nature I more strove to soothe,
With long forbearance, kindness, courtesy,
Than his who fell by me. But he disgraced me,
Stain'd me,—oh, death, and shame!—the world
          look'd on,
And saw this sinewy savage strike me down;
Rain blows upon me, drag me to and fro,
On the base earth, like carrion. Desperation,
In every fibre of my frame, cried vengeance!
I left the room, which he had quitted. Chance,
(Curse on the chance!) while boiling with my
          wrongs,
Thrust me against him, darkling in the street:—
I stab'd him to the heart:—and my oppressor
Roll'd, lifeless, at my foot.

    Wilf. Oh! mercy on me!
How could this deed be cover'd!

                   Mort.

Mort. Would you think it?
E'en at the moment when I gave the blow,
Butcher'd a fellow creature in the dark,
I had all good men's love. But my difgrace,
And my opponent's death, thus link'd with it,
Demanded notice of the magiftracy.
They fummon'd me, as friend would fummon friend,
To acts of import, and communication.
We met: and 'twas refolved, to ftifle rumour,
To put me on my trial. No accufer,
No evidence appear'd, to urge it on.—
'Twas meant to clear my fame.—How clear it, then?
How cover it? you fay.—Why, by a Lie:—
Guilt's offspring, and its guard. I taught this breaft,
Which Truth once made her throne, to forge a lie;
This tongue to utter it.—Rounded a tale,
Smooth as a Seraph's fong from Satan's mouth;
So well compacted, that the o'er throng'd court
Difturb'd cool juftice, in her judgment-feat,
By fhouting " Innocence!" ere I had finifh'd.
The Court enlarged me; and the giddy rabble
Bore me, in triumph, home. Aye!—look upon
      me.—
I know thy fight aches at me.
  Wilf. Heaven forgive me!
I think I love you ftill:—but I am young;
I know not what to fay:—it may be wrong.—
Indeed I pity you.
  Mort. I difdain all pity.—
I afk no confolation. Idle boy!
Think'ft thou that this compulfive confidence
Was given to move thy pity?—Love of Fame
(For ftill I cling to it) has urged me, thus,
To quafh thy curious mifchief in it's birth.
Hurt honour, in an evil, curfed hour,
Drove me to murder—lying:—'twould again.

       I   My

My honefty,—fweet peace of mind,—all, all !
Are barter'd for a name. I *will* maintain it.
Should flander whifper o'er my fepulchre,
And my foul's agency furvive in death,
I could embody it with heaven's lightning,
And the hot fhaft of my infulted fpirit
Should ftrike the blafter of memory
Dead in the church-yard. Boy, I would not kill
          thee :
Thy rafhnefs and difcernment threaten'd danger :
To check them there was no way left but this :—
Save one—your death :—you fhall not be my victim.
    Wilf. My death ! What take my life ?—My
          life ! to prop
This empty honour.
    Mort. Empty ! Groveling fool !
    Wilf. I am your fervant, Sir : child of your
          bounty ;
And know my obligation. I have been
Too curious, haply ; 'tis the fault of youth.
I ne'er meant injury : if it would ferve you,
I would lay down my life ; I'd give it freely :—
Could you, then, have the heart to rob me of it ?
You could not ;—fhould not.
    Mort. How !
    Wilf. You dare not.
    Mort. Dare not !
    Wilf. Some hours ago you durft not. Paffion
          moved you ;
Reflection interpofed, and held your arm :
But, fhould reflection prompt you to attempt it,
My innocence would give me ftrength to ftruggle,
And wreft the murderous weapon from your hand.
How would you look to find a peafant boy
Return the knife you level'd at his heart ;
And afk you which in heaven would fhew the beft,
                              A rich

A rich man's honour, or a poor man's honefty?

Mort. 'Tis plain I dare not take your life.   To
        fpare it,
I have endanger'd mine.   But dread my power;—
You know not it's extent.   Be warn'd in time:
Trifle not with my feelings.   Liften, Sir!
Myriads of engines, which my fecret working
Can roufe to action, now encircle you.
I fpeak not vaguely.   You have heard my prin-
        ciple;
Have heard, already, what it can effect:
Be cautious how you thwart it.   Shun my brother;
Your ruin hangs upon a thread: Provoke me,
And it fhall fall upon you.   Dare to make
The flighteft movement to awake my fears,
And the gaunt criminal, naked and ftake-tied,
Left on the heath to blifter in the fun,
'Till lingering death fhall end his agony,
Compared to thee, fhall feem more enviable
Than Cherubs to the damn'd.

    Wilf. O, mifery!
Difcard me fir!   I muft be hateful to you.
Banifh me hence.   I will be mute as death;
But let me quit your fervice.

    Mort. Never.—Fool!
To buy this fecret, you have fold yourfelf.
Your movements, eyes, and, moft of all, your
        breath,
From this time forth, are fetter'd to my will.
You have faid, truly: you are hateful to me:—
Yet you fhall feel my bounty:—that fhall flow,
And fwell your fortunes; but my inmoft foul
Will yearn with loathing, when—hark! fome one
        knocks!
Open the door.

                    I 2   [Wil-

[Wilford *opens the door, and* Winterton *comes in.*]

　Mort. How now, Winterton?
Did you knock more than once? Speak—did you
　　　　liften—
—I mean, good Adam, did you wait?—Aye, wait
Long at the door, here?
　Wint. Blefs your honour! no.
You are too good to let the old man wait.
　Mort. What, then, our talk, here—Wilford's
　　　　here and mine—
Did not detain you at the door?—Ha!—did it?
　Wint. Not half a fecond.
　Mort. Oh!—well, what's the matter?
　Wint. Captain Fitzharding, Sir, entreats your
　　　　company.
I've placed another flaggon on the table.
Your worfhip knows it.—Number thirty-five:—
The fupernaculum.
　Mort. Well, well.—I come.
What, has he been alone?
　Wint. No—I've been with him.
Od! he's a merry man! and does fo jeft!
He calls me firft of men, caufe my name's Adam.
Well! 'tis exceeding pleafant, by St. Thomas!
　Mort. Come, Adam; I'll attend the Captain.
　　　　—Wilford,
What I have juft now given you in charge,
Be fure to keep faft lock'd. I fhall be angry,—
Be very angry if I find you carelefs.
Follow me, Adam.
　　　　(Exit. Mortimer—Winterton *following.*
　Wilf. This houfe is no houfe for me. Fly I
will, I am refolved:—but whither? His threats
ftrike terror into me; and, were I to reach the pole,
I doubt whether I fhould elude his grafp. But to
　　　　　　　　　　　　　　　　live

live here a flave—flave to his fears,—his jealoufies!
Night's coming on. Darknefs be my friend! for
I will forth inftantly. The thought of my innocence will cheer me as I wander thro' the gloom.
Oh! when guilty Ambition writhes upon its couch,
why fhould bare-foot Integrity repine, though it's
fweet fleep be canopied with a ragged hovel!

(*Exit.*

SCENE V.—*The infide of an Abbey, in ruins.
Part of it converted into an habitation for Robbers.
Various entrances to their apartment, through the
broken arches of the building,* &c. &c.

Enter JUDITH, *and a* BOY.

Jud. Well, firrah! have you been upon the
fcout? Are any of our gang returning?

Boy. No, Judith! not a foul.

Jud. The rogues tarry thus to fret me.

Boy. Why, indeed, Judith, the credit of your
cookery is loft among thieves. They never come
punctual to their meals.

Jud. No tiding of Orfon yet, from the market
town?

Boy. I have feen nothing of him.

Jud. Brat! thou doft never bring me good news.

Boy. Judith, you are ever fo crofs with me!

Jud. That wretch Orfon flights my love of
late. Hence, you hemp-feed, hence! Get to
the broken porch of the abbey, and watch. 'Tis
all you are good for.

Boy. You know I am but young yet, Judith!
but with good inftructions, I may be a robber, in
time.

Jub.

Jud. Away, you imp! you will never reach such preferment. (*A whiftle without.*) So! I hear fome of our party. (*Whiftle again; the boy puts his fingers in his mouth, and whiftles in anfwer.*

Jud. Why muft you keep your noife, firrah?

Boy. Nay, Judith, 'tis one of the firft fteps we boys learn in the profeffion. I fhall ne'er come to good, if you check me fo. Huzza! here come two!

Enter two ROBBERS, *through the broken part of the Scene.*

Jud. So! you have found your road at laft. A murrain light upon you! is it thus you keep your hours?

1ft. Rob. What, hag, ever at this trade! Ever grumbling?

Jud. I have reafon. I toil to no credit; I watch with no thanks. I trim up the table for your return, and no one returns in due time to notice my induftry. Your meat is fcorch'd to cinders. Rogues, would it were poifon for you!

2d. Rob. How the fury raves! Here, take my carbine; 'twas levell'd, fome half hour fince, at a traveller's head.

Jud. Hah, hah, hah, Rare! Didft fhoot him?

1ft Rob. Shoot him? No. This devil in petticoats thinks no more of flaying a man, than killing a cock-chafer. I never knew a woman turn to mifchief, that fhe did not outdo a man, clean.

Jud. Did any of you meet Orfon on your way?

1ft Rob. Aye, there the hand points. When that fellow is abroad you are more favage than cuftomary; and that is needlefs.

2d Rob.

2d Rob. None of our comrades come yet? They will be finely foak'd.

1ſt Rob. Aye, the rain pours, like a ſpout, upon the ruins of the old abbey, wall here.

Jud. I'm glad on't. My it drench them, and breed agues! 'twill teach them to keep time.

1ſt. Rob. Peace, thou abominable railer! A man had better dwell in purgatory, than have thee in his habitation.—Peace, devil! or I'll make thee repent.

Jud. You! 'tis as much as thy life is worth to move my ſpleen.

1ſt. Rob. What, you will ſet Orſon, your champion upon me?

Jud. Coward! he ſhould not diſgrace himſelf with chaſtiſing thee.

1ſt Rob. Death and thunder!——

Jud. Aye, attack a woman, do! it ſuits your hen-hearted valour. Aſſault a woman!

1ſt Rob. Well—paſſion hurried me. But I have a reſpect for the ſoft ſex, and am cool again. Come Judith, be friends.—Nay, come, do; and I will give thee a farthingale, I took from a lawyer's widow.

Jud. Where is it?

1ſt Rob. You ſhall have it.

Jud. Well—I——Hark!

2d Rob. Soft! I think I hear the foot of a comrade.

MUSICAL DIALOGUE AND CHORUS.

ROBBERS and JUDITH.

Liſten! No; it is the owl,
That hoots upon the mould'ring tow'r.
Hark! the rain beats, the night is foul;
Our comrades ſtay beyond their hour.

Liſten!

Liften !
All's hufh'd around the abbey wall.————
Soft! Now I hear a robber's call !
Liften !
They whiftle !---Anfwer it !---'Tis nigh !
Again ! A comrade comes. ——'Tis I !
And here another; and here another !
Who comes? A brother. Who comes?
A brother.
Now they all come pouring in;
Our jollity will foon begin.
Sturdy partners, all appear !
We're here ! and here, and here, and here !
Thus we ftout freebooters prowl,
Then meet to drain the flowing bowl !

*(At different periods of the Mufick, the Robbers enter,
through various parts of the Ruins, in groups.*

Enter ORSON, *with Luggage on his Back, as if return'd from Market.*

1ft. *Rob.* See ! hither comes Orfon at laft. He
walks in like Plenty, with provifion on his fhoulder.

Jud. O, Orfon !—why did'ft tarry, Orfon? I
began to fear. Thou art cold and damp. Let
me wring the wet from thy cloaths. O ! my
heart leaps to fee thee.

1ft *Rob.* Mark how this fhe-bear hugs her
bruin !

Orf. Stand off ! this hamper has been weari-
fome enough. I want not thee on my neck.

Jud. Villain ! 'tis thus you ever ufe me. I can
revenge :—I can——do not, dear Orfon ! do not
treat me thus.

Orf. Let a man be ever fo fweet temper'd, he
will meet fomewhat to four it. I have been vex'd
to madnefs.

2d *Rob.* How now, Orfon, what has vex'd
thee now ?

Orf.

Orſ. A prize has ſlipt through my fingers.

3d Rob. Aye! marry, how?

Orſ. I met a ſtraggling knave on foot, and the rogue reſiſted. He had the face to tell me that he was thruſt on the world to ſeek his fortune; and that the little he had about him was his all. Plague on the proviſion at my back! I had no time to rifle him:—but I have ſpoil'd him for fortune-ſeeking, I warrant him.

Rob. How?

Orſ. Why I beat him to the ground. Whether he will e'er get up again the next paſſenger may diſcover.

Jud. Ha! Ha! O, brave! That's my valiant Orſon!

3d Rob. Orſon, you are ever diſobeying our Captain's order. You are too remorſeleſs, and bloody.

Orſ. Take heed, then, how you move my anger, by telling me on't. The affair is mine—I will anſwer to the conſequence.

4th Rob. I hear our Captain's ſignal. Here he comes. Ha!—he is leading one who ſeems wounded.

Enter ARMSTRONG, *ſupporting* WILFORD.

Arm. Gently, good fellow! come, keep a good heart!

Wilf. You are very kind. I had breathed my laſt, but for your care. Wither have you led me?

4th Rob. Where you will be well treated, youngſter. You are now among as honourable a knot of men as ever cried "ſtand" to a traveller.

Wilf. How: among robbers!

4th Rob. Why ſo the law's cant calls us gentlemen, who live at large.

K *Wilf.*

Wilf. So! For what am I referved!

Arm. Fear nothing. You are fafe in this afylum. Judith, lead him in. See fome of my linen ready, and look to his wound.

Jud. I do not like the office. Your are ever at thefe tricks. 'Twill ruin us in the end. What have we to do with charity?

Arm. Turbulent wretch! obey me.

Jud. Well, I fhall. Come, fellow, fince it muft be fo.

Arm. Anon, I'll vifit you myfelf, lad.

Wilf. Heaven blefs you! whate'er becomes of my life - and faith, I am almoft weary on't—I am bound to your charity. Gently, I pray you—my wound pains.—Gently!

(*Exit. led out by* JUDITH.

Arm. I would I knew which of you had done this.

1ft. Rob. Why what's the matter, Captain?

Arm. Cruelty is the matter. Had not accident led me to the fpot where he lay, yon poor boy had bled to death. I learn'd his ftory, partly, from him, on the way: and know how bafely he has been handled by one of you. Well, time muft difcover him: for he, who had brutality enough to commit the action, can fcarcely have courage enough to confefs it.

Orf. Courage, Captain, is a quality, I take it, little wanted by any here. What fignify words— I did it.

Arm. I fufpected thee, Orfon. 'Tis fcarce an hour fince he, whom thou haft wounded, quitted the fervice of Sir Edward Mortimer, in the foreft. here; and inquiry will doubtlefs be made.

2d. Rob. Nay then we are al difcover'd.

Arm. Now, mark what thou haft done. Thou

haft

haft endanger'd the fafety of our party; thou haft broken my order ('tis not the firft time, by many) in attacking a paffenger:—and what paffenger? One whofe unhappy cafe fhould have claim'd thy pity. He told you he had difpleafed his mafter—left the houfe of comfort, and with his fcanty pittance, was wandering round the world to mend his fortune. Like a butcher, you ftruck the forlorn boy to the earth, and left him to languifh in the foreft. Would any of our brave comrades have done this?

All.—None! None!

Arm. Comrades, in this cafe, my voice is fingle. But if it have any weight, this brute, this Orfon, fhall be thruft from our community, which he has difgraced. Let it not be faid, brothers, while want drives us to plunder, that wantonnefs prompts us to butchery.

Robbers. O brave Captain! away with him!

Orf. You had better ponder on't, ere you provoke me.

Arm. Rafcal! do you mutter threats? You cannot terrifye us. Our calling teems with danger—we are not to be daunted by the treachery of an informer. We defye you. Go. You dare not hurt us. You dare not facrifice fo many brave, and gallant fellows, to your revenge, and proclaim yourfelf fcoundrel. Begone.

Orf. Well, if I muft, I muft. I was always a friend to you all: but if you are bent on turning me out—why—fare you well.

Robbers. Aye, aye—Away, Away!

Orf. Farewell, then.   (*Exit.*

Arm. Come, comrades—Think no more of this. Let us drown the choler we have felt in wine and revelry.

FINALE.

FINALE.

Jolly Friars tippled here.
Ere thefe Abbey walls had crumbled;
Still the ruins boaft good cheer,
Though long ago the cloifters tumbled.
The Monks are-gone!——
Well! well!
That's all one:——
Let's ring their knell.
Ding dong! ding dong! to the bald-pated monk!
He fet the example,
We'll follow his fample,
And all go to bed moft religioufly drunk.
Peace to the good fat Friar's foul!
Who, every day,
Did wet his clay,
In the deep capacious bowl.
Huzza! Huzza! we'll drink and we'll fing!
We'll laugh, and we'll quaff,
And make the welkin ring!

END OF THE SECOND ACT.

ACT III.

SCENE I.—Winterton's *Room, in* Sir Edward Mortimer's *Lodge.*

Samson *and* Blanch, *discover'd, at a Table, with Bottles and Glasses.*

Blanch. SAMSON, you must drink no more.

Samf. One more glass, Mistress Blanch, and I shall be better company. 'Twill make me loving.

Blanch. Nay, then, you shall not have a drop.

Samf. I will:—and so shall you too. *(filling the glass)* Who knows but it may make you the same,

Blanch. You are wond'rous familiar, Mr. Lout.

Samf. I would not willingly offend. I will endeavour at more respect. My humble duty to you. *(drinks.)*

Blanch. I would counsel you to be cautious of drinking, Samson. Consider where you are. We are now, remember, in Sir Edward Mortimer's Lodge.

Samf. In the Butler's room;—where drinking has always a privilege. *(fills.)*

Blanch. What, another!

Samf. Do not fear. 'Twill not make me familiar again. My lowly respects to you. *(drinks)*

This

This fame old Winterton's wine has a marvellous choice flavour. I wonder whether 'twas fmuggled.

Blanch, Should you totter with this, now, in the morning, 'twould go nigh to fhake your office to the foundation, before night. My Lady would never pardon you.

Samf. 'Twould be hard to turn me adrift, for getting drunk, on the fecond day of my fervice.

Blanch. Truly, I think 'twould be reafon fufficient.

Samf. 'Twould not be giving a man a fair trial. How fhould fhe know but I intend to be fober for a year after?

Blanch. How fhould fhe know, indeed! or any one elfe, who has heard of your former rogueries.

Samf. Well, the worft fault I had was being a fportfman.

Blanch. A fportfman! out on you, rogue! you were a poacher.

Samf. Aye, fo the rich nick-name us poor brothers of the field; and lay us by the heels when we do that for hunger which they practice for amufement. Cannot I move you to take a thimble-full, this cold morning?

Blanch. Not a drop, I.

Samf. Hark! I think I hear old Winterton coming back. By our lady, Miftrefs Blanch, we have made a defperate hole in the bottle, fince he left us.

Blanch We! why, you flanderous rogue, I have not tafted it.

Samf. No—'tis not he.

Blanch. No matter; he will be back on the inftant. Leave this idle guzzling, if you have any fhame. Think we are attending madam Helen, in her vifit to Sir Edward, on his fudden ficknefs.

Think;

Think, too, on the confufion from Wilford's flight. Is it a time for you, fot, to tipple, when the whole houfe is in diftrefs and melancholy?

Samf. Alas! I have too tender a heart, Miftrefs Blanch; and have need of fomewhat, in the midft of this forrow, to cheer my fpirits.

Blanch. This wine will fhortly give your profeffions of amendment the lie.

Samf. Let it give me the lie: 'Tis an affront I can.eafily fwallow. Come, a bargain—an you will take one glafs with me, I will give over.

Blanch. Well, on that condition——

Samf. Agreed—for that will juft finifh the bottle. *(fills)* I will drink no health, now, but of thy giving.

Blanch. Then liften and edifye.—May a man never infult a woman with his company, when drunkennefs has made him a brute.

Samf. With all my heart:—But a woman knows that. man may be made a brute, when wine is clean out of the queftion. Eh! Here comes the old man in real earneft.

Enter ADAM WINTERTON.

Wint. Well, I am here again.—What madcap? —In truth, I have a world of care. Our good mafter taken ill, on the fudden. Wilford flown: —A bafe, ungrateful boy!—One that I was fo fond of:—And to prove fuch a profligate! I began to love the young villain like my own child. I had mark'd down the unfortunate boy, in my laft teftament: I had——Blefs me! my cold is wond'rous troublefome to my eyes, this morning. Ah! 'tis a wicked world:——But old Winterton
keeps

keeps a merry heart, ftill. Do I not, pretty miftrefs.
Blanch?

Blanch. I hope you do, Adam.

Wint. Nay, on fecond thought, I do not keep
it; for thou haft ftolen it from me, tulip! ha!
good ifaith!—

Samf. Ha! ha!—Well ifaith that is a good jeft!
ha! ha!

Wint. Doft think fo, varlet? " Thou haft ftolen it from me, tulip!" Well, it was; it was exceeding pleafant, by St. Thomas! Heigho! I
muft e'en take a glafs to confole me.   One cup to
——eh! mercy on me! why the liquor has flown.
Ha! the bottle has leak'd, haply.

Samf. Yes, Sir:—I crack'd that bottle, myfelf,
in your abfence.

Wint. Crack'd! Why what a carelefs goofe
art thou! thefe unthrifty knaves!—ah! times are
fadly changed, for the worfe, fince I was a boy.

Blanch. Doft think fo, Adam?

Wint. Queftion any man, of my age, and he
will fay the fame.   Domefticks never broke bottles in queen Elizabeth's time.   Servants were
better then—aye, marry, and the bottles were better bottles.   'Tis a degenerate world!   Well;
heigho!

Blanch. Why doft figh thus, Adam?

Wint. In truth, this is as heavy a day for me!—

Blanch. I hope not, Adam.   Come, come,
things are not fo bad, I warrant thee.   You have
long drank fmilingly of the cup of life, Adam;
and when a good man takes his potion without
murmuring, Providence feldom leaves the bitter-
eft drop at the bottom.   What is the matter,
Adam?

Wint.

Wint. Alas! nothing but evil. Thefe attacks come on our worthy mafter as thick as hail, and weaken him daily. He has been grievous ill, in the night, poor foul! and ne'er flept a wink fince I brought him the news.

Blanch. What news, good Adam?

Wint. Why of Wilford's flight.—A reprobate! The fhock of his bafenefs has brought on Sir Edward's old fymptoms.

Blanch. What call you his old fymptoms?

Wint. The fhiverings, and trembling fits, which have troubled him thefe two years. I begin to think the air of this foreft doth nourifh agues. I can never move him to drink enough of canary. I think, in my confcience, I had been aguifh myfelf, in thefe woods, had I not drank plenty of canary.

Samf. Mafs, when I am ill, this old boy fhall be my apothecary. *(afide.*

Blanch Well, well, he may mend. Do not fancy the worft, ere worfe arrives, Adam.

Wint. Nay, worfe has arrived, already.

Blanch. Aye! marry, how?

Wint. Wilford's villany. Sir Edward fays, he has proofs of the blackeft treachery againft him.

Blanch. Indeed!

Wint. It chills my old blood to think on't! I had mark'd out the boy as a boy of promife—A learned boy! He had the backs of all the books in our library by heart: and now a hue and cry is after him. Mercy on me! if the wretched lad be taken, Sir Edward will bring him to the charge. We none know what 'tis yet; but time will fhew.

Blanch. You furprife me! Wilford turn difhoneft! I could fcarce have credited this; and after two years trial, too.

Samf. O, monftrous! to turn rogue after two

L years

years trial! Had it happened after two days, indeed, 'twere not to be wonder'd at.

Enter a Servant.

Serv. Mr. Winterton, there is a young woman of the forest, would speak with you.

Wint. Out on't! These cottagers time their bufiness vilely. Well, bid her come in, Simon.

Serv. And, Miftrefs Blanch, your lady would fee you anon, in the breakfaft parlour.   *(Exit.*

Blanch. I come quickly. Be not caft down, now, Adam; keep thy old heart merry ftill.

Wint. Ha! in truth, I know not well, now, what would mend my fpirits.

Blanch. What think you of the kifs I promised?

Wint. Ah, wag! go thy way. Od! thou haft nimble legs. Had I o'ertaken thee yefterday——— Ah! well, no matter.

Blanch. Come, I will not leave thee comfortlefs, in thefe fad times. Here—Here is my hand, Adam.

Wint. Thou wilt fhew me a light pair of heels again, now.

Blanch. No, in faith. Come; 'tis more than I would offer to every one   Take it.

Wint. That I will, moft willingly. *(Kiffes her hand.)*

Blanch. Do not play the rake now, and boaft of my favours; for I am told there is a breed of puppies will build ftories, to a fimple girl's prejudice, on flighter encouragement than this. Be not you one of thofe empty coxcombs, and fo adieu, Adam.   [*Exit.*

Wint. Nay, I was never given to vaunt. 'Sbud! if I had, many a tale had been told, fixty years back,

of

of young, lufty Adam Winterton.—Eh! why what
doft thou titter at, fcapegrace?

Samf. I, fir?—Not I.　　　　*(fmothering a laugh.*

Wint. I had forgot this varlet. Peftilence on't!
Should this knave prate of my little gallantry, I
tremble for the good name of poor Miftrefs
Blanch!

Enter BARBARA.

Barb. May I come in, good your worfhip?

Wint. Aye, marry, that thou may'ft, pretty one.
—Well, though many things have declined, fince
I was a boy, female beauty keeps its rank ftill. I
do think there be more pretty women now than
there were in Queen Elizabeth's reign.

Samf. Flefh! this is our Barbara.　　*(afide.*

Wint. Well, and what wouldft have, fweet one,
with old Adam——Eh! by St. Thomas, why
thou art fhe I have feen, ere now, with Wilford.

Barb. Befeech you, tell me where he is, Sir.

Wint. Alas, child, he's gone—flown! Eh?
what—why, art not well, child?

Barb. Nothing, Sir——I only——I hoped
he would have called at our cottage, ere he quitted the foreft. Is there no hope that he may come
back, Sir?

Wint. None, truly, except force bring him back.
Alas, child! the boy has turn'd out naught; and
juftice is dogging him at the heels.

Barb. What Wilford, Sir?—my poor—O, Sir,
my heart is burfting! I pray you, pardon me.
Had he pafs'd our cottage in his flight, I would
have ran out, and follow'd him all the world over.

Wint. To fee what love will do! Juft fo did
Jane Blackthorn take on for me, when Sir Mar-

L 2　　　　　　　maduke

maduke carried me to London, in the hard winter.

Barb. Befeech you, forgive me, Sir! I only came to make inquiry, for I had heard a ftrange tale. I would not have my forrows make me troublefome to your worfhip.

Wint. To me? poor wench! nay, that thou art not. I truft, child, I ne'er turn'd a deaf ear, yet, to the unfortunate. 'Tis man's office to liften to the forrows of a woman, and do all he can to foothe them. Come, come, dry thy tears, chicken.

Barb. I look'd to have been his wife fhortly, Sir. He was as kind a youth——And, I am fure, he wanted not gratitude. I have heard him talk of you, as you were his father, Sir.

Wint. Did he? Ah! poor lad. Well, he had good qualities; but, alas! he is now a reprobate. Poor boy! To think, now, that he fhould fpeak kindly of the old man, behind his back!

Barb. Alas, this is the fecond flight to bring unhappinefs to our poor family!

Wint. The fecond! How do'ft mean, wench?

Barb. My brother, Sir, left our cottage fuddenly, yefterday morning; and we have no tidings of him fince.

Samf. Lo you, now, where he ftands, to glad the hearts of his difconfolate relations! Sifter Barbara, why doft not know me?

Barb. Eh! No—Sure it can't——Brother Samfon?

Samf. Mr. Samfon—Head ferving-man to the Lady Helen, of the New Foreft.

Barb. O, the fortune! can it be! what gain'd thee fo good a place, Samfon?

Samf.

Samf. Merit. I had no intereſt to back me. Mine is a rare caſe—I was promoted on the ſcore of my virtues.

Wint. Out upon thee! thy knaveries have been the talk of the whole foreſt; and furniſh'd daily food for converſation.

Samf. Truly, then, converſation has fared better upon them than I. But my old character is laid aſide, with my old jerkin. I am now exalted.

Wint. An I have any forecaſt, in deſtiny, friend, thou bidſt fair, one day, to be more exalted.— Ha! good ifaith! Come, you muſt to the kitchen, knave. I muſt thither myſelf, to give order for the day.

Barb. Muſt I return home, then, your worſhip, with no tidings?

Wint. Ah! heaven help me! what havock doth wanton Cupid make with us all! Well, tarry about the houſe, with thy brother; we may hear ſomewhat, haply, anon. Take care of thy ſiſter knave; and mark what I have ſaid to thee.—" Thou bidſt fair one day to be more exalted." Ha! well, it was exceeding pleaſant, by St. Thomas!

(*Exit.*

Samf. Well, Barbara, and how fares father?

Barb. He has done nought but chide, ſince you diſappear'd, Samſon. It has ſour'd him with us all.

Samf. Well, I will call, ſoon, and ſet all even.

Barb. Will you, brother?

Samf. I will. Bid him not be caſt down. I will protect the Rawbold family.

Barb. Truly, brother, we are much in need of protection.

Samf. Do not fear. Lean upon my power. I

am

am head of all the male domesticks, at madam
Helen's.

Barb. O, the father! of all! and how many be
there, brother?

Samf. Why, truly, not so many as there be at
the Lodge, here, But I have a boy under me, to
chop wood, and draw water.

Barb. The money we had from Sir Edward's
bounty, is nearly gone, in payment of the debt our
father owed. You know he had shortly been im-
prison'd, else.

Samf. My stock is somewhat low, too.—But,
no matter. Keep a good heart. I am now a
rising man. I will make you all comfortable.

Barb. Heaven bless you, Samson!

Samf. In three months, I look for a quarter's
wages; and then Dick shall have a shirt. I must
now take you roundly to task.

Barb. Me, brother!

Samf. Aye, marry. You would throw yourself away on this Wilford—who, as the story
goes, is little better than the devil's own imp.

Barb. O, brother! be not so uncharitable. I
know not what is against him, but he has not
been heard yet. Consider too—were all our actions, at home, to be sifted, I fear me, we might
not escape blameless.

Samf. Aye, but he, it seems, is falling, and
we are upon the rise; and that makes all the dif-
ference. Mass! how gingerly men will sift the
faults of those who are getting up hill in the
world; and what a rough shake they give those
who are going downward!

Barb. I would not be one of those sifters, brother.

Samf.

Samf. No,—I warrant, now, thou wouldſt marry this vagabond.

Barb. That I would, brother. He has cheer'd me in my diſtreſs, and I would ſooner die than leave him, now he is unfortunate.

Samf. Haſt thou no reſpect for the family? Thou wilt bring endleſs diſgrace on the name of Rawbold. Shame on you; to take away from our reputation, when we have ſo little!

Barb. I thought, brother, you would have ſhewn more pity for your poor ſiſter.

Samf. Tuſh! Love's a mere vapour.

Barb. Ah! brother.

DUET.

SAMSON *and* BARBARA.

I.

Barbara.

From break of the morning, were I with my love,
I'd talk till the evening drew nigh;
And, when the day did cloſe,
I'd ſing him to repoſe,
And tune my love a lullaby.

II.

Samſon.

From break of the morning, were I with my love,
O! long ere the evening drew nigh,
Her talk would make me doze,
Till the muſick of my noſe
Would play my love a lullaby.

III.

Barbara.

Our children around us, I'd look on my love,
Each moment in rapture would fly.

Samſon.

Samson.

But love is apt to pall,
When the brats begin to squall,
And a wife is screaming lullaby.

Both. From break of the morning. &c.   [*Exeunt.*

SCENE II. *A Room in Sir* EDWARD MORTI-MER's *Lodge.*

MORTIMER *and* HELEN *discover'd.*

Hel. Sooth, you look better now; indeed you do.
Mort. Thou'rt a sweet flatterer!
Hel. Ne'er trust me, then,
If I do flatter. This is wilfulness.—
Thou wilt be sick, because thou wilt be sick.
I'll laugh away this fancy, Mortimer.
  Mort. What couldst thou do to laugh away
            my sickness?
Hel. I'll mimick the physician—wise and dull—
With cane at nose, and nod emphatical,
Portentous in my silence; feel your pulse,
With an owl's face, that shall express as much
As Galen's head, cut out in wood, and gilt,
  Mort. And what wouldst thou prescribe?
Stuck over an apothecary's door.
  Hel. I would distil
Each flower that lavish happiness produced,
Through the world's paradise, ere Disobedience
Scatter'd the seeds of care; then mingle each,
In one huge cup of comfort for thee, love,
To chace away thy dulness. Thou shouldst wan-
      ton
Upon the wings of Time, and mock his flight,
                                        As

As he fail'd with thee tow'rd Eternity.
I'd have each hour, each minute of thy life,
A golden holiday; and fhould a cloud
O'ercaft thee, be it light as a goffamer,
That Helen might difperfe it with her breath,
And talk thee into funfhine!

    Mort. Sweet, fweet Helen!
Death, foften'd with thy voice, might dull his
    fting,
And fteep his darts in balfam. Oh! my Helen,
Thefe warnings which that grifly monarch fends,
Forerunners of his certain vifitation,
Of late are frequent with me. It fhould feem
I was not meant to live long.

    Hel. Mortimer!
My Mortimer! You——Oh! for heaven's fake,
Do not talk thus! You chill me. You are well;
Very well.—You give way—Oh, Mortimer!
Banifh thefe fantafies. Think on poor Helen!

    Mort. Think on thee, Helen?

    Hel. Aye: but not think thus.
You faid, my Mortimer, my voice could foothe,
In the moft trying ftruggle.

    Mort. Said I fo?
Yet, Helen, when my fancy paints a death-bed,
I ever place thee foremoft in the fcene,
To make the picture touching. After man
Is fummon'd, and has made up his account,
Oh! 'tis a bitter after-reck'ning, when
His pallid lips receive the laft, fad kifs,
Fond, female anguifh prints! Then, Helen, then,
Then comes man's agony! To leave the object
He fhelter'd in his heart, grief-ftruck, and help-
    lefs!
To grafp her hand; to fix his hollow eye
Upon her face, and mark her mute defpair,

          M   'Till

'Till the laft flutter of his aching fpirit
Hurries him hence, for ever!

Hel. Oh! for pity————
What have I done, that you———(*burfts into tears.*

Mort. My Helen!

Hel. I did not mean to weep. Oh, Mortimer,
I could not talk fo cruelly to you!
I would not pain you thus, for worlds!

Mort. Nay, come;
I meant not this. I did not mean to fay
There's danger now; but 'tis the privilege
Of ficknefs to be grave, and moralize
On that which ficknefs brings. I prithee, now,
Be comforted. Believe me, I fhall mend.
I feel I fhall, already.

Hel. Do you, Mortimer?
Do you, indeed, feel fo?

Mort. Indeed I do.

Hel. I knew you would:—I faid it. Did I not?
I am fo glad! You muft be cautious now.—
I'll play the nurfe to-day—and then, to-morrow,
You fhall not brood at home, as you are wont,
But we will ride together, through the foreft.
You muft have exercife. Oh! I will make you
Frefh as the fummer dew-drop, and as healthy
As ruddy Labour, fpringing from his bed,
To carol o'er the fallow!

Mort. Dearest prattler!
Men would meet ficknefs with a fmiling welcome,
Were all woo'd back to health thus prettily.

Hel. I fee it in your looks, now, you are better.

Mort. Scarce poffible, fo fuddenly!

Hel. O, yes;
There is no little movement of your face
But I can mark, on the inftant—'Tis my ftudy.
I have fo gazed upon it, that, I think,

I can

I can interpret ev'ry turn it has,
And read your inmost soul.

Mort. What?

Helen. Mercy on me!
You change again.

Mort. 'Twas nothing. Do not fear;
Thefe little fhocks are ufual.—'Twill not laft.

Helen. Would you could fhake them off!

Mort. I would I could!

Hel. Refolve it, then; and the bare refolution
Will bring the remedy. Rally your fpirits;
I prithee, now, endeavour.—This young man,
This boy—this Wilford—he has been ungrateful;
But do not let his bafenefs wear you thus.
Ev'n let him go.

Mort. I'll hunt him through the world!

Hel. Why, look you there now! Pray be calm.

Mort. Well, well;
I am too boifterous: 'Tis my unhappinefs
To feem moft harfh where I would fhew moft kind.
The world has made me peevifh.—This fame boy
Has fomewhat moved me.

Hel. He's beneath your care.
Seek him not now, to punifh him. Poor wretch!
He carries that away, within his breaft,
Which will embitter all his life to come,
And make him curfe the knowledge on't.

Mort. The knowledge!———
Has he then breathed———Carries within his
breaft!
What does he know?

Hel. His own ingratitude.

Mort. O, very true.

Hel. Then leave him to his confcience.
It is a fcorpion, fent by Heaven itfelf,
To fix on hidden crimes; a flow, ftill ftream,

M 2 Of

Of moulten lead, kept dropping on the heart,
To ſcald, and weigh it down. Believe me, love,
There is no earthly puniſhment ſo great,
To ſcourge an evil act, as man's own conſcience,
To tell him he is guilty.

 Mort. 'Tis a hell!
I pray you talk no more on't.—I am weak—
I did not ſleep laſt night.

 Helen. Would you ſleep now?

 Mort. No, Helen, no. I tire thy patient ſweet-
   neſs.

 Helen. Tire me! nay, that you do not. You
   forget
How often I have ſat by you, and watch'd,
Fanning the buſy ſummer-flies away,
Leſt they ſhould break your ſlumbers. Who
   comes here?

   Enter WINTERTON.

What Winterton! How do'ſt thou, old acquaintance?
How do'ſt thou, Adam?

 Wint. Bleſs your goodneſs, well.
Is my good maſter better?

 Helen. Somewhat, Adam.

 Wint. Now, by our lady, I rejoice to hear it!
I have a meſſage————

 Helen. O, no buſineſs now!

 Wint. Nay, ſo I ſaid. Quoth I, his honour's
   ſick;
Perilous ſick! but the rogue preſs'd, and preſs'd;
I could refuſe no longer. Out upon them!
The varlets know old Winterton's good nature.
'Tis my weak ſide.

 Helen. Who has thus importuned you?

 Wint. To ſay the truth, a moſt ill-favour'd varlet.
            But

But he will fpeak to none but to his worfhip.
I think 'tis foreft bufinefs.
 Mort. O, not now:
Another time—to-morrow—when he will.
I am unfit.—They teafe me!
 Wint. Ev'n as you pleafe, your worfhip. I
   fhould think,
From what he dropt, he can give fome account
Of the poor boy.
 Mort. Of Wilford!
 Wint. Troth, I think fo.
The knave is fhy; but Adam has a head.
 Mort. Quick; fend him hither on the inftant!
   Hafte!
Fly, Adam, fly!
 Wint. Well now, it glads my heart
To hear you fpeak fo brifkly.
 Mort. Well, defpatch!
 Wint. I go. Heaven blefs you both! Heaven
   fend you well,
And merry days may come again.   (*Exit.*
 Hel. I fear, this bufinefs may diftract you, Mor-
   timer:
I would you would defer it, till to-morrow.
 Mort. Not fo, fweet. Do not fear. I prithee,
   now,
Let me have way in this. Retire awhile.
Anon I'll come to thee.
 Hel. Pray now, be careful.
I dread thefe agitations. Pray, keep calm.
Now do not tarry long. Adieu, my Mortimer!
 Mort. Farewel, awhile, fweet!
 Hel. Since it muft be fo—
Farewel!   [*Exit Helen.*
 Mort. Dear, fimple innocence! thy words of
   comfort
             Pour

Pour oil upon my fires. Methought her eye,
When firſt ſhe ſpake of conſcience, ſhot a glance
Like her dead uncle on me. Well, for Wilford!
That ſlave can play the Parthian with my fame,
And wound it while he flies. Bring him before me,
Place me the runagate within my gripe,
And I will plant my honour on its baſe,
Firmer than adamant, tho' hell and death
Should moat the work with blood! Oh, how
      will ſin
Engender ſin! Throw guilt upon the ſoul,
And, like a rock daſh'd on the troubled lake,
'Twill form its circles, round ſucceeding round,
Each wider than the———

Enter ORSON.

How now! What's your buſineſs?
   Orſ. Part with your office in the foreſt: part
Concerns yourſelf in private.
   Mort. How myſelf?
   Orſ. Touching a ſervant of your houſe; a lad,
Whoſe heels, I find, were nimbler than his duty.
   Mort. Speak; what of him? Quick—Know
      you where he is?
Canſt bring me to him?
   Orſ. To the very ſpot.
   Mort. Do it.
   Orſ. Nay, ſoftly.
   Mort. I'll reward you—amply—
Enſure your fortunes.
   Orſ. Firſt enſure my neck.
'Twill do me little good elſe. I've no heirs;
And, when I die, 'tis like the law will bury me,
At its own charge.
   Mort. Be brief, and to your purpoſe.

                            Orſ.

Orf. Then, to the bufinefs which concerns your
   office,
Here, in the foreft.

Mort. Nay, of that anon.
Firft of my fervant.

Orf. Well, ev'n as you pleafe.
'Tis no rare thing—Let publick duty wait,
Till private interefts are fettled. But
My ftory is a chain. Take all together,
'Twill not unlink.

Mort. Be quick then. While we talk,
This flave efcapes me.

Orf. Little fear of that.
He's in no plight to journey far to-day.

Mort. Where is he hid ?

Orf. Hard by ; with robbers.

Mort. Robbers !———
Well, I'm glad on't. 'Twill fuit my purpofe beft.
            (*afide.*

—What, has he turn'd to plunder ?

Orf, No ; not fo.
Plunder has turn'd to him. He was knock'd down,
Laft night, here in the foreft, flat and fprawling ;
And the milk-hearted captain of our gang
Has fhelter'd him.

Mort. It feems, then, thou'rt a thief?

Orf. I ferved in the profeffion : But, laft night,
The fcurvy rogues cafhier'd me. 'Twas a plot,
To ruin a poor fellow in his calling,
And take away my means of getting bread.
I come, now, in revenge. I'll hang my comrades,
In clufters, on the forefts oaks, like acorns.

Mort. Where lyes their haunt ?

Orf. Give me your honour, firft———

Mort. I pledge it, for your fafety.

              Orf.

Orf. Send your officers
To the old abbey ruins; you will find
As bold a gang as e'er infested woods,
And fatten'd upon pillage.

Mort. What, so near me!
In some few minutes, then, he's mine! Ho!
Winterton!
Now for his lurking place! Hope dawns again.
Remain you here! I may have work for you.
(*to Orson.*

O! I will weave a web so intricate,
For this base insect! so entangle him!——
Why, Winterton! Thou jewel, Reputation!
Let me secure thee, bright and spotless, now,
And this weak, care-worn body's dissolution,
Will cheaply pay the purchase! Winterton!
[*Exit.*

Orf. There may be danger in my stay here. I
will e'en slink off, in the confusion I have raised.
I value not the reward. I hang my comrades, and
that shall content me.
(*Exit.*

A Hall in the Lodge.

Enter FITZHARDING.

Fitz. Rare scuttling tow'rd! This lodge is lit-
tle Babel:
And Spleen and Sickness are the household gods,
In this, my brother's, castle of confusion.
The hue and cry is up! I am half tempted
To wish the game too nimble for the dogs,
That hunt him at the heels. Dishonest! Well,
I'll ne'er trust looks again. His face hangs out
A goodly sign; but all within, it seems,

Is

Is dirty rooms, ftale.eggs, prick'd wine, four beer,
Rank bacon, mufty beef, and tallow candles.
I'll be deceived no more.—I'll mix with none,
In future, but the ugly: honeft men,
Who can out-grin a Griffin; or the head
Carved on the prow of the good fhip the Gorgon.
I'm for carbuncled, weather-beaten faces,
That frighten little children, and might ferve
For knockers to hall-gates.—Now—who are you?

Enter SAMSON.

Sam. Head ferving-man to madam Helen, Sir,
    Fitz. Well, I may talk to thee; for thou doft
            anfwer
To the defcription of the fort of men
I have refolved to live with.
    Sam. I am proud, Sir,
To find I have your countenance.
    Fitz. Can'ft tell me
The news of Wilford?
    Sam. He is turn'd a rogue, Sir.
An errant knave, Sir.   'Tis a rare thing, now,
To find an honeft fervant:—We are fcarce.
    Fitz. Where lyes the Abbey, where they go to
            feek him?
Doft know it?
    Sam. Marry, do I; in the dark.
I have ftood near it, many a time, in winter,
To watch the hares, by moonlight.
    Fitz. A cold paftime!
    Sam. Aye, Sir; 'twas killing work.   I've left
            it off.
    Fitz. Think you they will be back foon?
    Sam. On the inftant:
It is hard by, Sir.—Hark! I hear their horfes.
They are return'd, I warrant.

N   *Fitz.*

Fitz. Run you, fellow,——
If Wilford's taken, fend him here, to me.

Sam. Why he's a rogue, Sir. Would your
　　worſhip ſtoop
To parley with a rogue!

Fitz. Friend, I will ſtoop
To prop a ſinking man, that's call'd a rogue,
And count him innocent, 'till he's found guilty.
I learn'd it from our Engliſh laws; where Mercy
Models the weights that fill the ſcales of Juſtice;
And Charity, when Wiſdom gives her ſentence,
Stands by to prompt her. 'Till detection comes,
I ſide with the accuſed.

Sam. Would I had known
Your worſhip ſooner. You're a friend, indeed!
All undiſcover'd rogues are bound to pray for
　　you:
—So, Heaven bleſs you!

Fitz. Well, well—buſtle; ſtir:——
Do as I bid thee.

Sam. Aye Sir.—I ſhall lean
Upon your worſhip in my time of need.—
Heaven reward you!——Here's a friend to make!
　　　　　　　　　　　　　　(*Exit.*

Fitz. I have a kind of movement, ſtill, for
　　Wilford,
I cannot conquer. What can be this charge
Sir Edward brings againſt him?—Should the boy
Prove guilty!—well; why ſhould I pity guilt?
Philoſophers would call me driv'ler.—Let them.
Whip a deſerter, and Philoſophy
Sands by, and ſays he merits it. That's true:—
But wherefore ſhould Philoſophy take ſnuff,
When the poor culprit writhes? A plague on
　　Stoicks!
I cannot hoop my heart about with iron,
　　　　　　　　　　　　　　　Like

Like an old beer-butt. I would have the veſſel
What ſome call weak:—I'd have it ooze a little.
Better compaſſion ſhould be ſet abroach,
'Till it run waſte, then let a ſyſtem-monger
Bung it with Logick; or a trencher cap
Bawl out his ethics on it, 'till his thunder
Turns all the liquor ſour.—So! Here he comes!

Enter WILFORD.

Wilf. I am inform'd it is your pleaſure, Sir,
To ſpeak with me.
    Fitz. Aye, Wilford. I am ſorry—
Faith, very ſorry,—you and I meet thus.
How could you quit my brother thus abruptly?
Was he unkind to you?
    Wilf. Moſt bountiful.
He made me all I am. The poor can nnmber
His virtues thick as ſtars. I owe him, Sir,
A world of gratitude·
    Fitz. 'Tis a new mode
Of payment you have taken. Wherefore fly?
    Wilf. I was unfit to ſerve him, Sir.
    Fitz. Unfit!
    Wilf. I was unhappy, Sir. I fled a houſe
Where certain miſery awaited me,
While I was doom'd to dwell in't.
    Fitz. Miſery!
What was this certain miſery?
    Wilf. Your pardon,—
I never will divulge.
    Fitz. Indeed!
    Wilf. No, never.
Pray do not preſs me. All that I can ſay
Is, that I have a ſtrong, and rooted reaſon,
Which has reſolved me. 'Twere impoſſible
I ſhould be tranquil here. I feel it, Sir,

A duty

A duty to myself to quit this roof.

 Fitz. Harkye, young man. This smacks of
   myſtery;
And now looks foully. Truth, and Innocence,
Walk round the world in native nakedneſs;
But Guilt is cloak'd.

 Wilf. Whate'er the prejudice
My conduct conjures up, I muſt ſubmit.

 Fitz. 'Twere better now you conjured up your
   friends:
For I muſt tell you——No there is no need.
You learn'd it, doubtleſs, on the way, and know
The danger you, now, ſtand in.

 Wilf. Danger, Sir!
What? How? I have learn'd nothing, Sir; my
   guides
Drag'd me in ſilence hither.

 Fitz. Then 'tis fit
I put you on your guard. It grieves me, Wilford,
To ſay there is a heavy charge againſt you,
Which, as I gather, may affect your life.

 Wilf. Mine!—O, good Heaven!

 Fitz. Pray be calm:—for, ſoon,
Here, in the face of all his family,
My brother will accuſe you.

 Wilf. He!—What, He!
He accuſe *me*! O monſtrous! O, look down.
You who can read men's hearts!——A charge
   againſt me!
Ha, ha! I'm innocent! I'm innocent! *(much
  agitated.)*

 Fitz. Collect your firmneſs. You will need it
 all.

 Wilf. I ſhall, indeed! I pray you tell me, Sir,
What is the charge?

         Fitz.

Fitz. I do not know it's purport.
I would not hear on't: for on my voice rests
The iffue of this bufinefs;—and a judge
Should come unbiafs'd to his office. Wilford,
Were twenty brothers waiting my award,
You fhould have even, and impartial juftice.

Wilf. O, you are juft! I would all men were fo!

Fitz. I hope moft men are fo. Rally your
thoughts.
When you are call'd upon, if Truth will ferve
you,
Sketch out your ftory with her chafte, bold pencil:
If Truth fhould fail you, Wilford, even take
The faireft colours human art can mix,
To give a glow to plaufibility.
'Tis felf-defence; and 'tis allow'd, when man
Muft battle it, with all the world againft him.
——Heaven blefs you, boy!—that is, I mean—
pfhaw! plague!
—Farewell! and may you profper! *(Exit.*

Wilf. Then, all my youthful hopes are blighted
in the bud! The breath of my powerful perfecu-
tor will wither them. Let me recall my actions.
—My breaft is unclog'd with crime. This charge
is to be open;—in the eye of the world; of the
laws.—Then, why fhould I fear? I am native
of a happy foil where juftice guards equally the
life of its pooreft and richeft inhabitant. Let
him inflict his menaces upon me, in fecret; Let
him torture my mind and body; he fhall not,
cannot, touch my good name.

Enter

Enter BARBARA.

Barb. O, Wilford ! *(falls on his neck.)*

Wilf. Barbara ! at fuch a time, too !

Barb. To be brought back, thus, Wilford ! and to go away without feeing me; without thinking of me !

Wilf. It was not fo.—I was haftening to your cottage, Barbara, when a ruffian, in the foreft, encounter'd and wounded me.

Barb. Wounded you !

Wilf. Be not alarm'd. 'Tis not, as I thought yefternight, of moment. One of his party took me to the Abbey ruins, and gave me timely fuccour.

Barb. And, was it fo ! was it indeed fo, Wilford ?

Wilf. Aye, Barbara. When I was drag'd hither, the whole troop efcaped, or they had vouch'd for the truth on't.

Barb. I would they had not efcaped. For all here fay that you had fled to join them.

Wilf. What ! join with robbers ! what next fhall I be charged with !

Barb. Bethink you, Wilford—the time is fhort: I know your heart is good ; but————

Wilf. But what ? Can you fufpect it, too, Barbara !

Barb. O ! mine is fo link'd with it, that I would follow you through beggary, through prifons, Wilford.

Wilf. Prifons ! The found, now, makes me fhudder !

Barb. If in a hafty moment you have done
ought

ought to wrong Sir Edward, throw yourfelf on his mercy;—fue for pardon.

Wilf. For pardon!—I fhall go mad! Pardon! I am innocent.—Heaven knows I am innocent.

Barb. Heaven be thank'd—The family is all fummon'd. O, Wilford! my fpirits fink within me.

Wilf. (afide) I am, now, but a forry comforter.—Come, Barbara; be tranquil. You fee I am fo. Dont——dont you, Barbara? *(agitated)*

Enter a SERVANT.

Serv. You muft attend in the next room.

Wilf. What, Walter, is it you? Pray tell me if—

Serv. Do not queftion me. I hold no difcourfe with any of your ftamp.

Wilf. Your tone is ftrangely changed on the fudden. What have I done?

Serv. You are going to be tried. That's enough for me.

Wilf. I might rather claim your pity on that fcore, Walter.

Serv. What, pity a man that's going to be tried? O, monftrous!

Wilf. Well, fare you well. I will not upbraid you, Walter. You have many in the world to countenance you. Blacken well your neighbour, and nine in ten are in hafte to cry fhame upon him, ere he has time, or opportunity, to wipe off the accufation. I follow you.

Serv. Do fo.   *(Exit.*

Barb. O, Wilford!

Wilf. Be of good cheer. I go arm'd in honefty, Barbara. I can bear every thing. Every thing, fave making you the partner of my misfortunes.

That

That Barbara————I am fure you love me ————
that would give me a pang which would————
Farewell !   *(Exit.*

   Barb. Alas! I tremble for his fafety! fhould
they tear him from me !————

SONG.

BARBARA.

Down by the river there grows a green willow ;
  Sing all for my true love! my true love, O!
I'll weep out the night there, the bank for my pillow;
  And all for my true love, my true love, O!
When bleak blows the wind, and tempefts are beating.
I'll count all the clouds, as I mark them retreating,
For true lovers joys, well a-day! are as fleeting.
   Sing, O for my true love, &c.

Maids come, in pity, when I am departed!
  Sing all for my true love, &c.
When dead, on the bank, I am found broken-hearted,
  And all for my true love, &c.
Make me a grave, all while the wind's blowing,
Clofe to the ftream, where my tears once were flowing,
And over my corfe keep the green willow growing.
   'Tis all for my true love, &c.

                                    (Exit.

An Apartment in the Lodge.

FITZHARDING, WILFORD, *and various domefticks,*
  difcover'd.—To them enter ADAM WINTERTON.

  Fitz. Is not Sir Edward coming, Adam?
  Wint. Aye, Sir.—
But he is grievous ill.—Since Wilford came,
He had another fit.—But he'll be here.
Ah, boy! that I fhould live to fee this day!
I have a merry heart no longer, now.
  Wilf. Good man! you have been ever kind to
    me.

                                    Wint.

Wint. Heav'n fend you may prove honeſt!
　　Heaven fend it!
—Here comes Sir Edward. Would that I had
　　died
Two reigns ago!

Enter Sir Edward Mortimer.

Fitz. Now, brother.—You look pale,
And faint with ficknefs.
　　Wint. Here's a chair, your worſhip.
　　Mort. No matter.—To our buſinefs, brother.
　　　　Wilford,
You may well guefs the ſtruggle I endure
To place you here the mark of accuſation.
I gave you ample warning: Caution'd you,
When many might have fcourged: and, even now,
While I ſtand here to cruſh you,—aye, to cruſh
　　　　you,—
My heart bleeds drops of pity for your youth,
Whofe raſhnefs plucks the red deſtruction down,
And pulls the bolt upon you.
　　Wilf. You know beſt
The movements of your heart, fir. Man is blind,
And cannot read them : but there is a Judge,
To whofe all-feeing eye our inmoſt thoughts
Lye open. Think to him you, now, appeal.—
Omnifcience keeps Heaven's regiſter ;
And, foon or late, when Time unfolds the book,
Our trembling fouls muſt anfwer to the record,
And meet their due reward, or puniſhment.
　　Fitz. Now, to the point, I pray you.
　　Mort. Thus it is, then.
I do fufpect—By heaven, the ſtory lingers,
Like poifon, on my tongue,—but he will force
　　　　it—

O

Fitz.

Fitz. What is it you fufpect?

Mort. ——That he has rob'd me.

Wilf. Rob'd! I! O, horrible!

Fitz. Not yet—not yet.
Pray tell me brother—I will be impartial;—
But I am fomewhat moved.—Pray tell me, bro-
   ther,
How ground you this fufpicion?

Mort. Briefly, thus.——
You may have noticed, in my library,
A cheft *(Wilford ftarts)*—You fee he changes at
   the word.

 Wilf. And well I may!   *(afide.*

 Mort. Where I have told you, brother,
The writings which concern our family,
With jewels, cafh, and other articles,
Of no mean value, were depofited.

 Fitz. You oftentimes have faid fo.

 Mort. Yefterday,
Chance call'd me, fuddenly, away; I left
The key in't—but as fuddenly return'd;
And found this Wilford, this young man, whofe
   ftate,
Whofe orphan ftate, met pity in my houfe,
'Till pity grew to friendfhip,—him I found,
Fix'd o'er the cheft, upon his knees, intent,
As, now, I think, on plunder; tinging theft
Still blacker with ingratitude; and rifling
The eafy fool who fhelter'd him. Confufion
Shook his young joints, as he let fall the lid,
And gave me back the key.

 Fitz. Did you not fearch
Your papers on the inftant?

 Mort. No:—for, firft,
(Habit fo long had fix'd my confidence)
I deem'd it boyifh curiofity;—

        But

But told him this would meet my further queftion:
And, at that moment, came a fervant in,
To fay you were arrived.   He muft have mark'd
Our mix'd emotion.

 Fitz. Is that fervant here?

 Serv. 'Twas I, Sir.

 Mort. Was it you? Well, faw you ought
To challenge your attention?

 Serv. Sir, I did.
Wilford was pale, and trembling; and our mafter
Gave him a look as if 'twould pierce him through;
And cried, " Remember."—Then he trembled
   more,
And we both quitted him.

 Mort. When firft we met,
You found me fomewhat ruffled.

 Fitz. 'Tis moft true.

 Mort. But fomewhat more when, afterwards,
   I faw
Wilford converfing with you—like a fnake,
Sun'd by your looks, and bafking in your favour.
I bade him quit the room, with indignation,
And wait my coming in the library.

 Fitz. I witnefs'd that, with wonder.

 Mort. O, good brother!
You little thought, while you fo gently fchool'd
   me,
In the full flow of your benevolence,
For my harfh bearing tow'rd him, on what
   ground
That harfhnefs refted.   I had made my fearch,
In the brief interval of abfence from you,
And found my property had vanifh'd.

 Fitz. Well——
You met him in the library?

        Mort.

Mort. O never
Can he forget that folemn interview.

   Wilf. Aye, fpeak to that :—it was a folemn interview.

   Mort. Obferve, he does acknowledge that we
met.
Guilt was my theme:—he cannot, now deny it.

   Wilf. It was a theme of—No. *(checking himfelf.*

   Mort. He pleaded innocence :
While every word he fpake belied his features,
And mock'd his proteftation. I reftrain'd
The chaftifement he fear'd ; nor wou'd I blazon
The wrong I could not fix; and fubject, thus,
By general inquiry, all the guiltlefs
To foul fufpicion. That fufpicion lay
Moft heavily on him ; but the big cloud
Of anger he had gather'd burft not on him,
In vengeance, to o'erwhelm him : chill it drop'd,
But kindly, as the dew, in admonition ;
Like tears of fathers o'er a wayward child,
When love enforces them to ruggednefs.

   Fitz. What faid you to him?

   Mort. " Regulate your life,
" In future, better. I, now, fpare your youth;
" But dare not to proceed. All I exact,
" ('Tis a foft penance)—that you tarry here;
" My eye your guard, my houfe your gentle
         prifon,
" My bounty be your chains. Attempt not
         flight ;
" Flight ripens all my donbt to certainty,
" And juftice to the world unlocks my tongue."—
He fled, and I arraign him.

   Fitz. Truft me, brother,
This charge is ftaggering. Yet accidents
                      Some-

Sometimes combine to caft a fhade of doubt
Upon the innocent. May it be fo here!
Here is his trunk: 'twas brought here at my
    order.
'Tis fit that it be fearch'd.

    Mort. O, that were needlefs.
He were a fhallow villain that would truft
His freight of plunder to fo frail a bottom.
School-boys, who ftrip the orchard of its fruit,
Conceal their thievery better.

    Fitz. Yet 'tis found,
Such negligence is often link'd with guilt.
—Take note—I fay not yet that he is guilty;
But I fcarce heard of crafty villain, yet,
Who did not make fome blot in his foul game,
That lookers-on have thought him blind, and
          mad,
It was fo palpable.—'Tis rarely otherwife:
Heaven's hand is in it, brother: Providence
Marks guilt, as 'twere, with a fatuity.——
Adam, do you infpect it.   *(to Winterton.*

    Wilf. Here's the key—
E'en take it, freely.—You'll find little there
I value; fave a locket, which my mother
Gave me upon her death-bed; and fhe added
Her bleffing to't. Perhaps, her fpirit now
Is grieving for my injuries.

    Wint. (after opening the trunk). O, mercy!

    Fitz. How now? What's there?

    Wint. As I'm a wretched man,
The very watch my good old mafter wore!
And, here, my lady's jewels!

    Wilf. I am innocent.
Juft Heaven hear me!

    Fitz. I muft hear you, now.
What can you fay?—Oh! Wilford.

                           Wilf.

Wilf. Give me breath.
Let me collect myfelf. Firft this. *(fails on his*
knees)
                                 May fleep
Ne'er clofe my burning eyes; may confcience
        gnaw me;
May engines wrench my entrails from their feat;
And whirl them to the winds before my face,
If I know aught of this!
    Fitz. Make it appear fo.— But look there ; look
        there !   *(pointing to the trunk.*
    Wilf. Heap circumftance upon me ; multiply
Charge upon charge ; pile feeming fact on fact ;]
Still I maintain my innocence.   Look at me ;
Are thefe the throes of guilt? Are thefe convul-
        fions
Of a poor, helplefs, friendlefs, wretched boy,
The ftruggles of a villain ?—One thing more :
I here aver it—to his face aver it—
He knows—Yes, he—Yes, my accufer knows,
I merit not his charge.
              (a general expreffion of indignation)
    Wint. O! fie on't, fie !
    Fitz. Wilford, take heed ! A bafe attempt to
        blacken
An injured mafter, will but plunge you deeper,
    Wilf. I know what I am doing.   I repeat it :
Will die repeating it.   Sir Edward Mortimer
Is confcious of my innocence.
    Mort. Proceed——
Look at thefe proofs, and talk.—Unhappy boy,
Thy tongue can do me little mifchief, now.
    Wilf. Do you not know——
    Mort. What ?
    Wilf. ——'Tis no matter, fir.
But I could fwear——

                                 Mort.

Mort. Nay, Wilford, paufe a while.
Reflect that oaths are facred. Weigh the force
Of thefe affeverations. Mark it well.
I fwear, by all the ties that bind a man,
Divine or human! Think on that, and fhudder.
 Wilf. The very words I utter'd! I am tongue-
   tied.   *(afide.)*
 Fitz. Wilford, if there be aught that you can
   urge,
To clear yourfelf, advance it.
 Wilf. O, I could!
I could fay much, but muft not.—No, I will not.
Do as you pleafe.—I have no friend—no witnefs,
Save my accufer. Did he not—pray afk him—
Did he not vaunt his wiles could ruin me?
Did he not menace, in his pride of power,
To blaft my name, and crufh my innocence?
 Fitz. What do you anfwer, Sir?
 Mort. I anfwer—No.—
More were fuperfluous, when a criminal
Oppofes empty volubility
To circumftantial charge. A ftedfaft brow
Repels not fact, nor can invalidate
Thefe dumb, but damning, witneffes, before him.
      (pointing to the trunk.)
 Wilf. By the juft Pow'er that rules us, I am
   ignorant
How they came there!—but 'tis my firm belief,
You placed them there, to fink me.
 Fitz. O, too much!
You fteel men's hearts againft you! Death and
   fhame!
It roufes honeft choler. Call the officers.—
He fhall meet punifhment. *(Servants going.)*
         Mort.

Mort. Hold! pray you, hold.
Justice has, thus far, struggled with my pity,
To do an act of duty to the world.
I would unmask a hypocrite; lay bare
The front of guilt, that men may see, and shun it:
'Tis done—and I will, now, proceed no further.
I would not hurt the serpent, but to make
The serpent hurtless.   He has lost his sting.
Let him depart, and freely.
    Fitz. Look ye, brother.
This shall not be.—Had he proved innocent,
My friendship had been doubled; you well know
I have been partial to him—but this act
Is so begrimed with black, ungrateful malice,
That I insist on justice.   Fly, knaves! run,
And let him be secured.   [*Exeunt servants.*] You
        tarry here.   (*to Wilford.*)
    Mort. I will not have it thus.
    Fitz. You must—You shall—
'Tis weak else.   Oons! I trust I have as much
Of good, straight-forward pity, as may serve;
But, to turn dove—to sit still, and be peck'd at,
It is too tame.   His insolence tops all!
Does not this rouse you, too?—Look on these
        jewels.————
Look at this picture.—'Twas our mother's: Stay,
Let me inspect this nearer.   What are here?
Parchments————   (*inspecting the trunk.*)
    Mort. O, look no further—They are deeds,
Which, in his haste, no doubt, he crowded there,
Not knowing what—to look o'er at his leisure—
Family deeds—They all were in my chest.
    Wilf. O, 'tis deep laid!—These, too, to give a
        colour!   (*aside.*)
                                        Fitz.

Fitz. What have we here? I have your leave, good brother,
As arbiter in this. Here is a paper
Of curious enfolding—flipt, as 'twere
By chance, within another. This may be
Of note upon his trial.———What's this drops?
A knife, it feems!

Mort. What! *(ftarting.)*

Fitz. Marks of blood upon it.

Mort. Touch it not. Throw it back!—bury
it—fink it!
Oh, carelefsnefs and hafte! Give me that paper.
Darknefs and hell!—Give back the paper.

> [MORTIMER *attempts to fnatch it;* WILFORD
> *runs between the two brothers, falls on his
> knees, and prevents him, holding* FITZHARD-
> ING.]

Wilf. (*rapidly*) No.
I fee—I fee!—Preferve it. You are judge!—
My innocence, my life, refts on it!

Mort. Devils,
Foil me at my own game!—Fate!—Ha, ha, ha!
Sport, Lucifer!———He ftruck me———

> [MORTIMER *is fainting, and falling;* WIL-
> FORD *runs and catches him.*]

Wilf. I'll fupport him.———
Read! read! read!

Fitz. What is this?—My mind mifgives me!
It is my brother's hand!—*To die before me!*
What can this mean?——— [*reads.*]
Narrative of my murder of——Oh, great Heav'n!
" If by fome chance my guilt fhould be difclofed,

" May this contribute to redeem the wreck
" Of my loft honour!"—I am horror-ftruck!
Wilf. Plain, plain!————Stay! he revives.
Mort. What has been———— foft!
I have been wand'ring with the damn'd, fure.—
     Brother!—
And—aye—'tis Wilford. Oh! thought flafhes
     on me.
Like Lightning. I am brain-fcorch'd. Give me
     leave.
I will fpeak—Soon I will——a little yet———
Come hither, boy.—Wrong'd boy! O Wilford,
     Wilford!
     (*burfts into tears, and falls on Wilford's neck.*)
Wilf. Be firm, Sir; pray be firm! my heart
     bleeds for you—
Warms for you! Oh! all your former charity
To your poor boy, is in my mind.—Still, ftill,
I fee my benefactor.
     Mort. Well, I will—
I will be firm. One ftruggle, and 'tis over.
I have moft foully wrong'd you! Ere I die—
And I feel death-ftruck—let me hafte to make
Atonement.—Brother, note. The jewels,
Yes, and that paper—Heaven and accident
Ordain'd it fo!—were placed—Curfe on my flefh,
To tremble thus!—were placed there by my hand.
     Fitz. O, mercy on me!
     Mort. More. I fear'd this boy;
He knew my fecret; and I blacken'd him,
That, fhould he e'er divulge the fatal ftory,
His word might meet no credit. Infamy
Will brand my mem'ry for't: Pofterity,
Whofe breath I made my god, will keep my fhame
Green in her damning record. Oh! I had—
                              I had

I had a heart o'erflowing with good thoughts
For all mankind! One fatal, fatal turn,
Has poifon'd all! Where is my honour, now?
To die!—To have my afhes trampled on,
By the proud foot of fcorn! Polluted! Hell—
Who dares to mock my guilt? Is't you—or you?
—Wrack me that grinning fiend! Damnation!
Who fpits upon my grave? I'll ftab again—
I'll——Oh!   (*falls.*)
    Fitz. This rives my heart in twain. Why,
        brother, brother!
His looks are ghaftly.

Enter SERVANT.

    Serv. Sir, the officers.
    Fitz. Away, knave! Send them hence—the
        boy is innocent.
    Serv. What, Wilford?
    Fitz. Aye. Tell it your fellows. Hence!—
You fhall know more anon. Send in fome help—
Your mafter's ill o' the fudden. Send fome help!
                    (*Exit Servant.*
    Wilf. 'Twere beft to raife him, Sir.
    Fitz. Soft, who comes here?

Enter HELEN.

    Helen. Where is he? Ill! and on the ground!
        Oh, Mortimer!
Oh, Heaven! my Mortimer. O, raife him.—
        Gently.
Speak to me, love. He cannot!
    Mort. Helen—'Twas I that———
    (*he ftruggles to fpeak, but appears unable to utter.*)
                    Helen.

Helen. Oh, he's convulfed!

Fitz. Say nothing. We muft lead him to his chamber.

Befeech you to fay nothing! Come, good lady.

(FITZHARDING *and* HELEN *lead* MORTIMER *out.*)

Enter BARBARA, *on the oppofite fide.*

Barb. O, Wilford! I have flown to you! You are innocent.——The whole houfe now has it, you are innocent. Thank Heaven! Speak; tell me——How——how was it, dear, dear Wilford?

Wilf. I cannot tell you now, Barbara. Another time: But it is fo.——I cannot fpeak now.——

Barb. Nor I, fcarce, for joy. See! hither come your fellows, to greet you. I am fo happy!

Enter SERVANTS, *&c. &c. &c.*

Servants. Joy! Wilford.

Wilf. Peace, peace, I pray you. Our mafter is taken ill: So ill, my fellows, that I fear me, he ftands in much danger. That you rejoice in my acquittal, I perceive, and thank you. Sir Edward's brother will explain further to you: I cannot. But believe this:——Heaven, to whofe eye the dark movements of guilt are manifeft, will ever watch over, and fuccour the innocent, in their extremity. Clamour not now your congratulations to me, I entreat you: Rather, let the flow, ftill voice of gratitude be lifted up to Providence, for that care fhe ever beftows upon thofe deferving her protection!

FINALE.

FINALE.

Where Gratitude fhall breathe the note,
  To white-robed Mercy's throne,
Bid the mild ftrain on æther float,
  A foft and dulcet tone.

Sweet, fweet and clear the accents raife,
While mellow flutes fhall fwell the fong of praife.
    Melody! Melody!
    A foft and dulcet melody!

Where fever droops his burning head;
Where fick men languifh on their bed;
    Around let ev'ry accent be,
      Harmony! Harmony!
    A foft and dulcet harmony!

THE END.

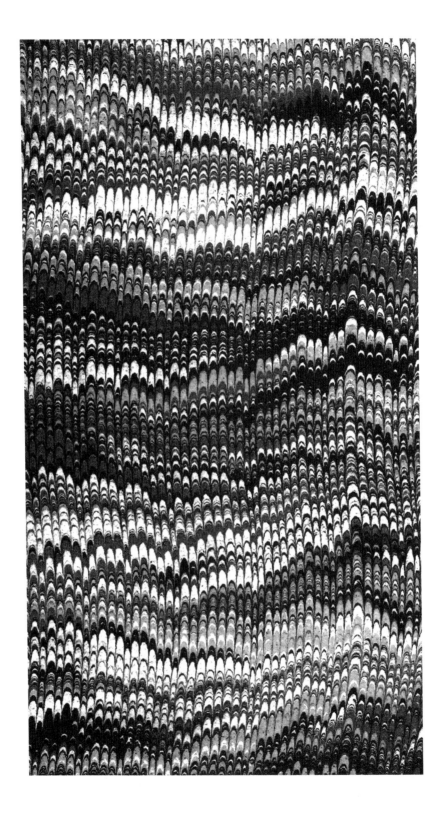

CPSIA information can be obtained
at www.ICGtesting.com
Printed in the USA
LVOW03s0219050116

469060LV00016B/655/P